THE BOOK OF PASSOVER

THE BOOK OF PASSOVER

A Celebration

Rabbi Benjamin Blech

CITADEL PRESS
Kensington Publishing Corp.
www.kensingtonbooks.com

CITADEL PRESS BOOKS are published by

Kensington Publishing Corp.
850 Third Avenue
New York, NY 10022

Copyright © 2005 Benjamin Blech

All Kensington titles, imprints, and distributed lines are available at special quantity discounts for
bulk purchases for sales promotions, premiums, fund-raising, educational, or institutional use.
Special book excerpts or customized printings can also be created to fit specific needs. For details,
write or phone the office of the Kensington special sales manager: Kensington Publishing Corp.,
850 Third Avenue, New York, NY 10022, attn: Special Sales Department; phone 1-800-221-2647.

CITADEL PRESS and the Citadel logo are Reg. U.S. Pat. & TM Off.

Illustrations by Mitchell Cramer
Book design by Anne Ricigliano/Planet Patti Inc.

10 9 8 7 6 5 4 3 2 1

Printed in the United States of America

Library of Congress Control Number: 2004095832

ISBN 0-8065-2580-0

This book will be a legacy to your future, creating memories
for the generations to come.

Please dedicate it here to someone you love:

Why is this book different than any other book?

Because you are invited to become a coauthor.

You'll learn a lot about Passover, the most important family holiday for the Jewish people—and you'll also have an opportunity throughout these pages to add your own comments.

CONTENTS

THE BOOK OF PASSOVER

The Story of a Seder Plate

The Meaning of Memories

This book was conceived in an antique store. It was while I was browsing for an item of Jewish interest in a little shop in lower New York. What I found made me weep. But I soon realized that tears weren't enough. It was then that I vowed to tell the story to others so as to ensure that nothing like it ever happens again.

You see, I was a witness to a murder. Not the murder of a person. No, perhaps something even more horrible. The murder of memory. The callous, cruel indifference to the most important message of the Passover holiday. And the irony was that the story revolved around the very symbol of Passover, the plate that is used for the traditional meal known as the Seder.

What I spotted in that antique store was a Seder plate that I immediately recognized. And how could I not? After all, it was the focus of my eulogy some years before for Sam, a survivor of the infamous Auschwitz concentration camp.

What a tale it had been. The Germans had rounded up all the Jews in his little town for deportation. Others may have believed the grand lie that they were merely being transported to another site to be used for labor. Sam was too smart for that. He knew that they meant to murder them. He understood that the Nazis wanted to eliminate every Jew as well as every reminder of their religious heritage. So Sam took a chance. Had he been caught, he would have paid with his life. But he did what he had to do in order that some remnant of his people might remain—so that even if not a single Jew in the world survived, someone might find it, and reflect and remember.

He wished he could have hidden much more. How he wanted to preserve a scroll of the Bible or a holy synagogue vessel. But he had so little time, so little space for concealing an object of value. His choice, in retrospect, seemed almost divinely inspired for its symbolism. It was a silver Passover plate used to commemorate the ancient festival of freedom.

Perhaps, Sam dared to hope, miracles could once more occur in modern times. And from that day forward, not a day went by in the hells of the concentration camps that his mind did not return to his Seder plate in its special hiding place, buried exactly fifty paces from his favorite tree in his back yard. For him, the tree took on the significance of the biblical "tree of life" in the Garden of Eden. If ever he could retrieve this link with his God and his people, he would foil the German plan to destroy every remnant of Judaism. The Passover story would have a modern-day sequel; Hitler's "Final Solution" would be overcome by the treasure guarded by his very own tree of life.

Sam could never explain how he of all his family and friends survived. In his heart of hearts, he once confided to me, it may have been because he viewed his continued existence on earth as a holy mission—to go back to his home and uncover his own symbol of survival.

Incredibly enough, Sam was eventually reunited with his ritual reminder of deliverance from age-old Egyptian oppression. He retrieved his Seder plate and lived to celebrate dozens of Passovers with it until his death.

And that very Seder plate, incredibly enough, is what I saw in the shop for sale!

Where was it from, I inquired? How did the owner come to have it? Oh, I was told, it was part of the sale of the contents of an estate by the children. "You see, the deceased was religious but his descendants aren't—so they don't really have any need for items like these." The buried treasure of the past had become the discarded trash of the generation that followed.

Indeed, this wasn't the first time I discovered that we live in an age that doesn't understand the meaning of memories or the concept of keepsakes. How I wish that the unsentimental cynicism of Sam's descendants were just an aberration, a remarkably unusual demonstration of insensitivity unlikely to be duplicated by others. But the sad truth is that we're part of a "throwaway" culture that gives equal weight to used cars, worn furniture, and old family heirlooms. What has served the past is of no interest if its sole claim to respectability is its gift of mental associations.

"Unless we remember," English novelist Edward Morgan Foster put it so beautifully, "we cannot understand." The past leaves its messages robed in the simplest of garments. They are the soul of those very things with which we come into daily contact. And they possess the unique ability of stirring up memories that keep alive those whom we deeply loved.

Dishes on which we shared festive meals. Pictures we looked at together and understood in a way no one else did. The silver cup my father gave me when he told me I was "now a man," and he expected great things of me. The trinkets we purchased that summer we always call the best vacation of our lives. The first toy we bought for our children. How can such inexpensive objects bring me so much pleasure—or sadness? It is foolish to think of what we have as possessions. We do not own them as much as they have a claim on us.

Every so often the newspapers carry a story of a rummage sale that brings a surprised buyer unexpected riches. Unwittingly someone sells a valuable painting for a pittance, an irreplaceable antique, and a one-of-a-kind object. The frustrated owner bemoans the fact that he was unaware of the object's true value. But what makes him unhappy is only the knowledge that he could have gotten more money for it. The world's valuation is what shocks him. Yet he still fails to realize that so much more of what he gave away for pennies had priceless worth for him if he would have but taken the time to see it. "The heart hath its own memory, like the mind," Longfellow taught us, "and in it are enshrined the precious keepsakes."

Memorabilia have lost their allure because we no longer revere the meaning of memories. So what, I am often asked, if my grandparents used this every holiday? We have no space; we have no need for it. As if utilitarian function is the only rationale for holding on to something that enables us to preserve our past!

The ring with which I married my wife may not be the most expensive, but I pray it remains in my family as a legacy of the love we shared, perhaps to be used again by my grandchildren. The small cup with which I usher in the sanctity of every Sabbath may reflect the poverty of my youth, but I hope that my family passes it on to the future as a testament to the importance of religious values in our household.

If children hold what we treasured sacred, then perhaps what we lived for will also be reverentially recalled. After all, memories, as Jewish tradition teaches us, are God's way of granting us immortality. That's because what we remember we keep alive. And that is an idea God considered so important that He turned it into the very first Jewish holiday.

Why do Jews celebrate Passover? Of course it commemorates a miracle. Yes, our ancestors were delivered from the bondage of Egypt. But that happened a long time ago, over 3,500 years ago. Why should we still care? Why should we bother with all the rituals that seem to have no contemporary relevance? Why insist that our children sit with us at a Seder discussing events of thousands of years past?

The answer is simple: *What we are doing is creating memories.* Not in the synagogue, but in our homes. Not with strangers, but with family and friends. Not to listen to a rabbi or cantor, but to be like rabbis and cantors ourselves—to lead a service of our very own, sharing our original insights into the Passover story. Retelling the past in a way that binds us to the future. Making our children the focus of our attention as we listen to them "ask the questions." On the very first Passover, we became a people; how appropriate that every Passover since then we ensure our survival and become reborn through the power of memory.

"Remember," the Bible commands us, because memory *is the secret of eternal life.* It is why the Jewish people have survived throughout the ages. And it is how our parents and grandparents live on in us, even as we hope to live on in the hearts of our descendants. This book was written so that none of us will ever suffer the fate of Sam who survived the fierce hatred of his enemies but not the forgetfulness of his loved ones.

What you will find in these pages is a prescription for memories. In a way, this is a family album, an album not of pictures but of words. It will get you to think about your connection with the past, and it will let you record the image you want to leave of yourself for the future. Throughout the book you will have a chance to note your own reactions and to write your own legacy to your children and grandchildren.

Please pass this book over to the next generation so that they'll not only remember what you *look* like from your photos but truly know what you *are* like from your comments. Then Passover will really have fulfilled its purpose—to create a link of love and understanding between the generations.

Memories

God gave us memories that we might have roses in December.
—Sir James M. Barrie

A scattered nation that remembers its past and connects it with the present will undoubtedly have a future as a people and probably even a more glorious life than the one in the past. —Lev Levanda

We do not remember days; we remember moments. —Cesare Pavese

So live that your memories will be part of your happiness.
—Author unknown

Life brings simple pleasures to us every day. It is up to us to make them wonderful memories. —Cathy Allen

Memories are the key not to the past, but to the future.
—Corrie Ten Boom

Every man's memory is his private literature.   —Aldous Huxley

Memories are all we really own.   —Elias Lieberman

> There are candles that remember
>   for twenty-four hours,
>
> As the label says. And there are candles
>   that remember for eight hours,
>
> And there are eternal candles that promise
> The memory of a man to his sons.
>
> —Yehudah Amichai

Why Passover Is Such a Beloved Jewish Holiday

People Love Passover Because . . .

Passover is more than a holiday. Passover is the magical message of spring, the season Thoreau called "an experience in immortality." It is the time when Mother Nature reminds us that rebirth and rejuvenation are part of God's plan for the world; flowers that perish in fall return in full bloom, and no winter lasts forever.

Passover is the biblical proclamation that human beings are meant to be free; that slavery is not to be tolerated because God has made all of us equal, in His image.

Passover is the birthday of the Jewish people, when the descendants of Abraham, Isaac, and Jacob were redeemed from Egypt and chosen by God to begin their role as His chosen people who would serve as "a light unto the nations."

Passover is the wonder of ritual, the beauty of ceremony, the power of customs, the spirituality of tradition, the meaningfulness of shared observance. In its most memorable moment, at the Passover Seder, it transmits religious values from generation to generation, from the past to the future.

Passover is a holiday that transforms us. The Seder makes us sacred by reminding us of our historic relationship with God. Its messages help us to become holy in the realization that all of our actions are judged by a heavenly Ruler of mankind who holds us responsible for our deeds. Of all the festivals of the year, it is no wonder that, like our first love, we probably love Passover the most.

Let's look at some of the most beautiful things about it:

People Love Passover Because . . .

On Passover, We Are Reminded That God Cares About Every Single One of Us

He demonstrated this when He spared every home of His people as He "passed over" their residences on the night He punished their oppressors. The Passover story is so important that it's given as the reason for the First of the Ten Commandments: "I am the Lord, your God, who took you out of the land of Egypt, the house of bondage." (Exodus 20:2)

Why, ask the commentators on the Bible, does God identify Himself as the One who took us out of the slavery of Egypt when He could have mentioned something far greater? Wouldn't it have been much more powerful for God to describe Himself as the One who created the heavens and the earth?

The answer is simple: to believe in God the Creator still doesn't make Him relevant to *me*. If God created the world and no longer has an intimate, ongoing relationship with it, why should I worship Him? If God doesn't care about me, why should I care about Him?

On the very first Passover, God showed us not just that He exists but that He continues to play a role in human history. *Passover proved that God is more than a passive bystander in our lives; because He loves us, we can always count on Him for protection, for guidance, and for salvation.* Whenever we celebrate the Festival of Freedom, we're filled with joy because we know that God takes a personal interest in our loved ones and us.

A Personal God

The Lord is near to all those who call upon Him.   —Psalms 145:18

God speaks to all individuals through what happens to them moment by moment.   —J. P. DeCaussade

God does not die on the day when we cease to believe in a personal deity, but we die on the day when our lives cease to be illuminated by the steady radiance, renewed daily, of a wonder, the source of which is beyond all reason.   —Dag Hammarskjöld

I know that God has been personally involved in my life because _____

_____

_____

_____

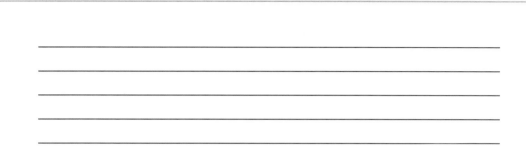

On Passover, We Are Reminded That God Performs Miracles

Whenever we are overwhelmed by personal problems that we think are insurmountable, we remember the story of our ancestors in Egypt. It was impossible for them to overcome the might of the world's major empire. It was impossible for them to realize their dream of freedom. It was impossible for them to escape when the Egyptian army trapped them at the shore of the Red Sea. It was impossible—except that God can and does perform miracles.

God can afflict evildoers with miraculous plagues. God can split the sea and allow us to cross on dry land. God can drown our enemies and let us sing a song of redemption.

And just as God performed all these wondrous things a long time ago, we know that to this day He's still performing miracles. They may be camouflaged as coincidence, but we've come to realize that coincidence is just God's way of choosing to remain anonymous.

Were a blind man suddenly to see, we would all pronounce it a miracle; so why do we take our vision for granted? Why don't we recognize God in the very fact of our existence? And why don't we realize that the same God who saved the Jews in the Passover story over three thousand years ago is still busy saving us from the perils that face us all the days of our lives?

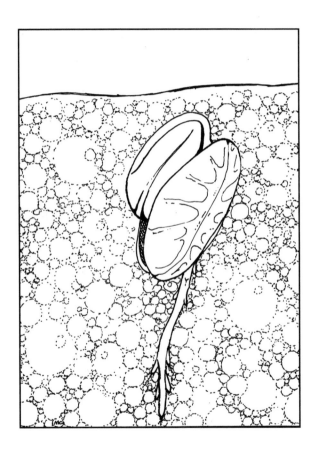

Miracles

The age of miracles is forever here.   —Thomas Carlyle

No man can share in the Torah of Moses unless he believes that all our affairs and events, concerning the masses or the individual, are miracles.
                                                —Nachmanides

Miracles are a retelling in small letters of the very same story that is written across the whole world in letters too large for some of us to see.
                                                —C. S. Lewis

Miracles are God's coups d'etat.   —Anne-Sophie Swetchine

In Israel, in order to be a realist you must believe in miracles.
                                                —Prime Minister Ben Gurion

The true miracle is not walking on water or walking in air, but simply walking on this *earth*.   —Thich Nhat Hanh

Don't believe in miracles—depend on them.   —Laurence J. Peter

There are only two ways to live your life. One is as though nothing is a miracle. The other is as though everything is a miracle.
                                                —Albert Einstein

For the truly faithful, no miracle is necessary. For those who doubt, no miracle is sufficient.   —Nancy Gibbs

To me every hour of the day and night is an unspeakably perfect miracle.   —Walt Whitman

All change is a miracle to contemplate; but it is a miracle which is taking place every second.   —Henry David Thoreau

I believe in miracles because _____

_____

_____

_____

_____

_____

_____

_____

_____

_____

_____

_____

On Passover, We Are Reminded of the Importance of Family

Passover commemorates the birth of the Jewish people. But remarkably enough the birth of the nation was preceded by God's emphasis on the primacy of the family. Before the Jews left Egypt, they were commanded to celebrate their forthcoming redemption. The first Seder took place the night before the exodus. God told Moses to instruct the people: "On the tenth day of this month, they shall take every man a lamb according to their father's houses, a lamb for a household" (Exodus 12:3).

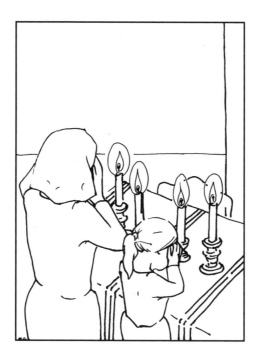

The very first divinely commanded ritual meal was observed in every household together with family. Wouldn't it have been better, some might wonder, for all Jews to have come together communally at some large gathering spot where they could collectively celebrate their imminent salvation? No, God had a different idea. The Jews had to first strengthen the ties of family before they could become His people. *A nation is only as strong as its family units.*

The secret of Jewish survival has always rested on this truth. That's why the Bible counted the ancient Israelites "according to their families, according to their households." And that's why, on the holiday that begins our historic mission, we observe the major ritual not in the communal house of worship but in the more sacred arena of our own homes. Tradition teaches us that God is happy when we visit Him in His Temple, but He's even happier when we invite Him into our homes.

Family

The family is one of nature's masterpieces.   —George Santayana

The family is the nucleus of civilization.   —William J. Durant

Call it a clan, call it a network, call it a tribe, call it a family: whatever you call it, whoever you are . . . you need one.   —Jane Howard

What families have in common the world around is that they are the place where people learn who they are and how to be that way.
　　　　　　　　　　　　　　　　　　　　　—Jean Illsley Clarke

Family life is full of major and minor crises . . the ups and downs
of health, success and failure in career, marriage, and divorce . . .
and all kinds of characters. It's tied to places and events and histories.
With all of these felt details, life etches itself into memory and
personality. It's difficult to imagine anything more nourishing to the
soul.   —Thomas Moore

There is one practice that any family can maintain and that is the
practice of a time of worship at each family meal. The table is really the
family altar!   —Elton Trueblood

My family means more than anything to me because_____

_____

_____

_____

_____

_____

_____

_____

_____

_____

On Passover, We Are Reminded of How Important It Is for Us to Spend Time with Our Children

In God's infinite wisdom, the Bible turned Passover into a holiday that forces us to sit down and have a real conversation with our youngsters. God knew that if the nation He was creating was to have a chance at continued existence, there would have to be dialogue between the generations.

So God made the central feature of the Seder, a commandment to "tell your children." In Hebrew, the word for "to tell" is *Higadeta*—and that's why the book that we read is called the Haggadah. Imagine! A law that demands we actually sit around a table *and talk to our kids*! How relevant for today when social critics point out that we've become a society where home is no more than the place strangers come to pick up the car keys. Communication is a lost art for couch potatoes who think togetherness is sitting close to each other while staring at the same television program.

Parents who can't find any time to share with their children, Judaism teaches, are no better off than slaves—and didn't God redeem us from Egypt so that we would no longer *be* slaves?

Children

A baby is God's opinion that life should go on.   —Carl Sandburg

Each day of our lives we make deposits in the memory banks of our children.   —Charles R. Swindoll

The soul is healed by being with children.   —Fyodor Dostoyevsky

Cherishing children is the mark of a civilized society.
                                    —Joan Ganz Cooney

At the end of your life, you will never regret not having passed one
more test, not winning one more verdict, or not closing one more deal.
You will regret time not spent with a husband, a friend, a child, or a
parent.   —Barbara Bush

The best inheritance a person can give to his children is a few minutes
of his time each day.   —O. A. Battista

I am my kid's mom.   —Dr. Laura Schlessinger

Your children are not your children. They are the sons and daughters
of Life's longing for itself. They come through you but not from you,
and though they are with you, yet they belong not to you.
                                    —Kahlil Gibran

Good parents give their children Roots and Wings. Roots to know
where home is, wings to fly away and exercise what's been taught them.
                                    —Jonas Salk

If a child is to keep his inborn sense of wonder, he needs the companionship of at least one adult who can share it, rediscovering with him the joy, excitement, and mystery of the world we live in.

—Rachel Carson

Perhaps the greatest social service that can be rendered by anybody to the country and to mankind is to bring up a family.

—George Bernard Shaw

A hundred years from now it will not matter what my bank account was, the sort of house I lived in, or the kind of car I drove . . . but the world may be different because I was important in the life of a child.

—Author unknown

I want to find more time to spend with my children so that_____

_____

_____

_____

_____

_____

_____

_____

Passover is my favorite holiday because _____

_____

_____

_____

_____

_____

_____

_____

_____

Some Biblical Highlights
of the Passover Story

It's So Interesting to Know . . .

The story is found in the Bible, in the book of Exodus. Everyone knows the basic plot, the main characters, the villains and the heroes.

Joseph, the favorite son of Jacob who had been sold into Egyptian slavery by his own brothers, rose to a position of leadership second only to King Pharaoh. Years later, famine forced the family of Jacob to settle in Egypt where they were reunited.

The Hebrews were at first warmly received, out of respect for Joseph's contributions to their economy. Egypt acknowledged Joseph as their nation's savior. They recognized that it was only due to his efforts that it became the leading world power.

But, as the Bible puts it, "A new king arose who did not remember Joseph." Ignoring any obligation of gratitude, the Egyptian ruler soon turned the people who saved the land into slaves. The oppressed children of Israel cried out to God, and with the help of their divinely appointed leader, Moses, their prayers were answered with a series of incredible miracles. Ten plagues afflicted the Egyptian slave masters, the last one taking the lives of their firstborn children, until the Egyptians literally chased the Hebrews out of their land in such haste that they didn't even have time "to let their bread rise."

On that night of the tenth plague, God smote every Egyptian home but He "Passed-over" the houses of His people where, in anticipation of their deliverance, the Hebrews were celebrating the first Seder in history.

That was the night when the dream of freedom became a reality. The date was the fifteenth of Nissan. And that is the very night we celebrate Passover throughout all of history, to remember with gratitude the miracles of our past and to affirm with full confidence our belief in God's ongoing help in the future.

It's So Interesting to Know . . .

How Moses Got His Name

When Pharaoh's daughter went to bathe in the Nile River, she spotted a child in a little ark floating in the water. Realizing that this was a Hebrew infant, she determined—as Schindler would do many years later during the Holocaust—that she would save at least one child from death, defying her own father's edict. After paying to have him nursed, she adopted him and called him Moses to serve as an everlasting reminder that, as his name means in the Hebrew, "from the water I drew him."

The rabbis point out that this wasn't the name Moses was given by his own parents. Yet throughout the ages Jews continue to refer to their greatest rabbi and leader

by the name chosen by a stranger who wasn't even Jewish! Why? *To show the importance of gratitude.*

Just as we must never forget the evil of those who sought to destroy us, we must never fail to recall the kindness of those who intervened to deliver us. Whenever we mention Moses by name, we're making a statement: Gratitude is so important, it's meant to be eternal.

Gratitude

Ingratitude to man is ingratitude to God.   —Samuel HaNagid

Is it not most shameful that, in requiting favors, man should be left behind by a dog?   —Philo

Feeling gratitude and not expressing it is like wrapping a present and not giving it.   —William Arthur Ward

Gratitude is not only the greatest of virtues, but the parent of all others.
                                                              —Cicero

Gratitude unlocks the fullness of life. It turns what we have into enough, and more. It turns denial into acceptance, chaos to order, confusion to clarity. It can turn a meal into a feast, a house into a home, a stranger into a friend. Gratitude makes sense of our past, brings peace for today, and creates a vision for tomorrow.
                                                    —Melody Beattie

To speak gratitude is courteous and pleasant, to enact gratitude is generous and noble, but to live gratitude is to touch Heaven.
                                                    —Johannes A. Gaertner

Gratitude is the heart's memory.   —French Proverb

God has two dwellings; one in heaven, and the other in a meek and thankful heart.   —Izaak Walton

In our daily lives, we must see that it is not happiness that makes us grateful, but the gratefulness that makes us happy.   —Albert Clarke

The best and most beautiful things in the world cannot be seen or even touched. They must be felt with the heart.   —Helen Keller

Let us be grateful to people who make us happy—they are the charming gardeners who make our souls blossom.   —Marcel Proust

O Lord that lends me life, lend me a heart replete with thankfulness!
—William Shakespeare

I want to always remember with gratitude the kindnesses these people showed me:

_____

_____

_____

_____

_____

_____

_____

_____

How God Appeared to Moses for the Very First Time

Moses was tending the sheep of his father-in-law in the desert of Sinai. Suddenly, he was amazed to see a bush that was burning and yet, miraculously, was not consumed. As he gazed at it in wonder, God appeared to him with the divine call to become the leader of the Jewish people.

But why did God have to bother with a bush on fire? Couldn't He simply have spoken to Moses? And if the point was to demonstrate divine power, couldn't God have come up with something more striking than a small plant that was able to resist destruction by fire?

The rabbis of old saw in this story a powerful symbol of the very miracle that would define the existence of the Jewish people throughout all of history. *Against all natural law, the Jewish people somehow survive; no matter how strong the fires set by their enemies, Jews are never consumed.*

Here is how Leo Tolstoy put it in wonderment: "A Jew is the emblem of eternity. He who has been for so long the Guardian of Prophecy and has transmitted it to the rest of the world—such a nation cannot be destroyed. The Jew is as everlasting as eternity itself." Indeed, the Jew is the miracle of the burning bush. And that's what God revealed to Moses at their very first encounter!

Why God Chose Moses to Be the Leader of the Jewish People

There are three little stories in the Bible that precede his divine call at the burning bush. What they all have in common is a vivid illustration of a character trait that defined his true greatness.

One day, Moses walked the grounds of the palace and saw an Egyptian smiting a Hebrew. Of course he could easily have moved on and ignored the evil taking place just a few feet before him. How simple for all of us just to say, "Well, that's none of my business." But Moses couldn't do that. Even though he wasn't personally threatened, his passion for justice forced him to intervene. At great personal risk, he punished the wicked and saved the life of the innocent.

On the very next day, he saw two Hebrews fighting. Perhaps, you will say, a quarrel between brothers doesn't call for outside intervention. But Moses didn't see it that way. Here, too, he separated the combatants and tried to make peace.

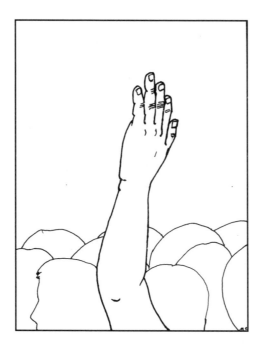

Finally, after moving to Midian, Moses witnessed a number of shepherds mistreating some girls who came to water their flock at the well. No matter that this injustice was perpetrated against total strangers: Moses once again came to the aid of the oppressed.

What made Moses worthy of being the Jewish leader? *A true leader is someone who is never content to sit back and mind his own business; as the Talmud puts it, to be involved is to become a partner with God in the act of Creation.*

Moses Suffered from a Speech Defect

Yes, the greatest rabbi of all time was "slow of speech and slow of tongue." It says so in the Bible! We're not sure if that means he had a lisp or a stutter. But whichever one it was, many people would surely have been quick to write off his prospects for leadership. The handicapped rabbi? God could certainly have found a more capable spokesman. Better yet, God could have easily cured Moses of his defect.

But God didn't do that. He allowed an "imperfect" Moses to represent Him in order to teach us an all-important lesson: Imperfections are nothing less than human steppingstones to greatness. Perhaps disabilities are even blessings in disguise. That's what Helen Keller realized when she contemplated how God had deprived her of sight and hearing: "Although the world is full of suffering, it is also full of the overcoming of it. . . . Character cannot be developed in ease and quiet. Only through experience of trial and suffering can the soul be strengthened, ambition inspired, and success achieved." So that's probably why God didn't cure Moses—because He wanted him to be able to become Moses!

Moses Is Described as the Most Humble of Men upon the Earth

When God came to Moses and told him he was chosen to lead the Jews out of Egypt, his first words were, "Who am I?" Moses simply didn't consider himself worthy of this honor. That wasn't just a gratuitous act. It was a natural expression of his character. Moses must have known that his abilities were far greater than those of other people. Yet even at the height of his career as leader, he continued to demonstrate this same trait of modesty.

How was that possible? Don't geniuses have a right to recognize their superiority over others? Not if we use Moses as our model. Moses understood that his unique talents were simply a gift from God. That doesn't make him better than other people. It merely makes him more blessed. How can anyone use divine favors as rationale for looking down at others?

Here is the advice given by the Talmud: "Learn from the Creator. He revealed Himself on Sinai, a low mountain, not on the heights; in a bush, and not on majestic trees. True wisdom can be found only among the humble."

And perhaps more people ought to remind themselves of the wisdom of the Italian proverb that asks us to reflect on our mortality: "Once the game is over, the king and the pawn go back in the same box."

Who Was Singled Out to Be the First One Smitten by Every Plague

Here's a great question to think about: When a nation commits a great crime, who is most guilty—the leader who planned it or the followers who actually carried it out? Think about any of the terrible events of the recent past. Should we demonize Hitler most of all—or are the real villains the German people? Were the excesses of the Communist regime the primary fault of Stalin or of his Soviet henchmen? Is it the head that dreams up the policy or the hand that executes it that deserves most to be punished?

True, both are at fault. Responsibility lies with the ruler as well as his messengers. But whose sin is greater? The Bible gives us the answer. *The sequence speaks to the level of guilt of the sinner.*

Moses and Aaron warned Pharaoh, "And the river shall swarm with frogs, which shall go up and come into *your* house and into *your* bedchamber, and upon *your* bed, and then into the house of your servants, and then into the houses of your servants and your people" (Exodus 7:28). The Pharaohs of the world are the ones who deserve the wrath of God more than anyone else. The political leaders who plot evil are far more dangerous than legions of armies. Today the cruelest tyrants seek political asylum. In the Bible, they were made to pay the price for their role in preparing the plans for their country's crimes.

The Condition for Being Saved

There was a special requirement for the Jews on the night that God "passed over" their homes, sparing their families as He slew the Egyptians' firstborn. On the very first Passover night, Jews celebrated the Seder while God passed through the land and executed judgment against all the firstborn of the Egyptians. Jews were saved from the lethal effects of this plague—but only on one condition. They had to identify their homes with the blood of a sacrificed lamb smeared on their doorpost. God warned the Jews: "And the blood shall be to you for a sign upon the houses where you are; and when I see the blood, I will pass over you, and there will be no plague upon you to destroy you, when I smite the land of Egypt" (Exodus 12:13).

Did God really need a sign for Him to know where Jews lived? Doesn't an all-knowing God have the ability to recognize Jewish homes without benefit of a blood marker? The rabbis teach us that God demanded the sign not for Himself but for us. *We needed to identify ourselves publicly as Jews in order to deserve to be saved.* The doorpost is our outer face to the larger world. Too many times in our history there have been those who knew they were Jews but sought to hide that from their neighbors. They were Jews by birth but not Jews by choice. Religion was for them a source of embarrassment rather than pride.

Those were the Jews God wouldn't save when He began an intimate and everlasting relationship with His people. To be worthy of God, Jews have to be willing publicly to proclaim their love for Him.

How the Red Sea Miraculously Split for the Jews
When the Egyptians Pursued Them

Cecil B. DeMille almost had it right in his classic film *The Ten Commandments*. Yes, the Jews stood paralyzed with fear on the shore of the Red Sea as they watched their former masters approaching. On one side, certain slaughter by the sword of the Egyptian army. On the other, unavoidable death by drowning. Moses lifts his hands with the staff of God—and behold the sea splits. A path leads directly through the

midst of the raging waters, allowing the Jews to march through to safety! But one part of the story in the movie is left out. For Jews it may very well be the most significant aspect of the miracle. God didn't split the sea *until the Jews walked into the water up to their necks.* It was only when it was impossible for the Jews to do any more on their own that God intervened.

The first miracle was the miracle of faith, a miracle performed by the Jews. We will trust in God, they said, no matter how hopeless it seems. Only then did God respond with a miracle. God made the impossible happen because we showed we believed He had the ability to do so. And that's how God to this day continues to perform miracles for all those who demonstrate their faith in Him!

Faith

Faith is the strength by which a shattered world shall emerge into the light.   —Helen Keller

Take the first step in faith. You don't have to see the whole staircase, just take the first step.   —Dr. Martin Luther King Jr.

I do not pray for success. I ask for faith.   —Mother Teresa

A little faith will bring your soul to heaven; A great faith will bring heaven to your soul.   —Charles Spurgeon

Without faith, nothing is possible. With it, nothing is impossible.
—Mary McLeod Bethune

Faith is an oasis in the heart that will never be reached by the caravan of thinking.   —Kahlil Gibran

He who loses money, loses much; he who loses a friend, loses much more; he who loses faith, loses all.   —Eleanor Roosevelt

You can do very little with faith, but you can do nothing without it.
—Samuel Butler

Faith walks simply, childlike, between the darkness of human life and the hope of what is to come.   —Catherine de Hueck Doherty

Faith is that quality or power by which the things desired become the things possessed.   —Kathryn Kuhlman

The righteous shall live by his faith.   —Bible, Habbakuk 2:4

I believe in the sun even when it is not shining. I believe in love even when not feeling it. I believe in God even when He is silent.
—Inscription in a Cologne cellar
where Jews hid from the Nazis

There were bad times in my life, but I never lost my faith when _____

_____

_____

_____

_____

_____

_____

_____

My own favorite part of the Passover story is _____

_____

_____

_____

_____

_____

_____

_____

Some Favorite Passover Folklore

It's So Fascinating to Learn . . .

The word *midrash* in Hebrew means searching. It is the name given to all the classic rabbinic interpretations of the Bible, spanning many hundreds of years, which were compiled around the beginning of the common era.

The books of *midrashim* include stories, folklore, history, and playful excursions into the world of the imagination. Some *midrashim* are intended to be taken literally, accepted as revealed truths handed down throughout the generations. Others are clearly metaphors meant as messages. They are the poetry of history. To read *midrashim* is to understand the soul of the Jewish people.

Passover night is a fitting time to recall the beautiful ideas implicit in these *midrashim*. They are the spiritual food for our Seder discussions. Scholars have pondered their significance throughout the ages. Do not be put off by their simplicity. Use them as springboards for conversations with your children about the meaning of life—its purpose, its pains, its pleasures, and its opportunities for personal growth and enrichment.

It's So Fascinating to Learn . . .

Egyptian Astrologers Accurately Predicted the Day on Which Moses Was Born

Experts in reading the stars, they foresaw the birth of a child who would liberate the Jewish people and wreak havoc on the Egyptian Empire. The ominous date, according to their calculations, was the seventh day of Adar, and so they warned Pharaoh to drown every male child, be he Egyptian or Jew, born on that day.

The astrologers very much wanted to be far more exact in their warning. It would certainly have been much better if they could have told Pharaoh to simply put to death every Hebrew child born on that day and spare the babies of their own people. But for reasons they could not understand, the astrologers were faced with an incomprehensible contradiction. They were getting mixed signals. On the one hand, they perceived this future usurper to be someone descended from the children of Israel. On the other hand, the astrologers saw from their readings that this revolutionary figure seemed to be Egyptian. To make sure that Pharaoh "got the right man," they advised, as the Bible tells us, "to throw into the Nile *every* male child"— even those born to Egyptian mothers.

Why was it, the *Midrash* wonders, that the astrologers could have been so prescient with regard to the very day and yet be so confused concerning Moses' national identity?

The answer, the *Midrash* explains, rests on a profound principle of Jewish law. A parent is defined as the one who gives birth to a child as well as the one who raises him. Moses of course was born of Hebrew parentage. But it was the daughter of

Pharaoh who later brought him up in the palace. That made him a product of two major life-giving sources. Biologically, Moses was a Jew. But by education and rearing, he was an Egyptian.

Jewish law demands that a child give honor both to the parents who bore him as well as to those who teach him and raise him. And that's why the astrologers couldn't figure out whether the redeemer of the Jewish people was really a Hebrew or an Egyptian—because in God's eyes, *he was both*!

Teachers

He who teaches a child is as if he gave birth to him.   —Talmud

Children owe respect to their parents because they brought them into this world. Children owe respect to their teachers because they bring them into the World to Come.   —Talmud

The dream begins with a teacher who believes in you, who tugs and pushes and leads you to the next plateau, sometimes poking you with a sharp stick called "truth."   —Dan Rather

In teaching you cannot see the fruit of a day's work. It is invisible and remains so, maybe for twenty years.   —Jacques Barzun

A teacher affects eternity; he can never tell where his influence stops.
—Henry Brooks Adams

The mediocre teacher tells. The good teacher explains. The superior teacher demonstrates. The great teacher inspires.   —William Arthur Ward

I dreamt I stood in a studio
And watched two sculptors there.

The clay they used was a young child's mind
And they fashioned it with care.

One was a teacher—the tools he used
Were books, music, and art.

The other, a parent, worked with a guiding hand
And a gentle loving heart.

Day after day, the teacher toiled
With touch that was deft and sure.

While the parent labored by his side
And polished and smoothed it o'er.

And when at last, their task was done
They were proud of what they'd wrought.

For the things they had molded into the child
Could neither be sold nor bought.

And each agreed they would have failed
If each had worked alone.
For behind the teacher stood the school
And behind the parent stood the home.

—Author unknown

There were a few teachers in my lifetime who, like my parents, were responsible for making me the person I am today. I want to remember them and what they mean to me: _____

_____

_____

_____

_____

_____

_____

_____

If It Weren't for His Sister Miriam, Moses Would Not Have Been Born

The *Midrash* tells us that when Pharaoh announced his decree of death for all boys to be born in his kingdom, Amrom, father of Miriam, publicly declared that in light of this harsh decree, he was going to separate from his wife. He would not continue to have sexual relations, since he in effect would be bringing children into a world in which they would be doomed to immediate demise. "I will not be a partner with Pharaoh in his evil plan," Amrom publicly announced. And because he was a much-respected Jewish leader, other Hebrews followed suit. Families were disbanded. Births were no longer possible. This seemingly sane response to a world gone mad implied collective national suicide.

It was then that Miriam dared to argue with her father. The younger generation understood something that the elders, in their despondency, could not grasp. With words that seem shocking, the *Midrash* tells us that Miriam criticized her father by way of this harsh rebuke: "My father, your decree is more severe than Pharaoh's. Pharaoh decreed only against the males, but you have decreed against the males and the females. Pharaoh only decreed concerning this world, but you have decreed concerning this world and the world to come, inasmuch as those children never born will certainly be denied the hereafter. In the case of the wicked Pharaoh, there is still doubt whether his decree will be fulfilled or not. Perhaps through a miracle, some child will escape. Yet, with your plan to end family relations, it is certain that the decree against Jewish survival will be fulfilled."

When there is a genocidal plan in effect against Jews, is there any point in still having children? Is pregnancy an absurd option in a time of a holocaust? Amrom was the pessimist. But the view of Miriam prevailed. Amrom admitted his daughter's logic had more merit, and he resumed marital relations with his wife. And that is how it came to pass that Moses was born.

Pessimism

I doubt anyone will ever see—anywhere—a memorial to a pessimist.
—Source unknown

Pessimism is a luxury that a Jew can never allow himself.
—Golda Meir

Pessimist's Definition of Optimism: Failing to learn from life.
Optimist's Definition of Pessimism: Failing to learn to live.
—Martijn Faassen

Pessimism is a contagious disease;
optimism is a miraculous medicine.
—William Arthur Ward

How the Hand of the Princess Miraculously Stretched

When the daughter of Pharaoh rescued Moses from the Nile, after he had been placed in the ark by his mother, God performed an incredible miracle. The daughter of Pharaoh understood that the little child had to be a Hebrew. She knew it must have been a mother's desperate attempt to save her baby, hoping against hope that somebody would take pity on him and raise the boy who was condemned to death.

The princess thousands of years ago carried out a plan that we recognize by way of a remarkable sequel in the twentieth century with the heroic deed of a German named Oskar Schindler. The daughter of Pharaoh couldn't undo her father's decree. She could, however, save just one life. And with that she understood, as Judaism would proclaim by way of one of its major teachings, that "whosoever preserves a single life is as though he had kept alive the whole world."

The princess did not dare to involve any of her handmaidens in her plot. She couldn't send someone to get the ark for her. Yet she knew she had to reach it. And so comes the incredible comment of the *Midrash*, the princess standing at the bank of the Nile, stretched out her hand—and her hand miraculously became elongated many, many hand breadths, so that she was able to reach the ark and retrieve it!

What an incredible rabbinic stretch of the imagination! Hands that reach out surely don't become physically lengthened. Yet, the rabbis insist that's precisely what happened! The message? Stretch out your hand to accomplish something even if it's impossible by natural law. Our responsibility is to reach out. With the help of God, we'll grasp what we seek—because God's outstretched arm will come to our aid.

Why the Princess Had to Find a Hebrew Woman to Nurse Moses

According to the *Midrash*, there is an amazing part to the story that didn't make it into the Bible. The princess wanted to adopt the baby she found. In order to have him fed, she searched for someone to nurse the child. But the task proved impossible. Candidate after candidate, nursing woman after nursing woman, attempted to breast-feed the infant Moses, only to have him turn his head away. What could it possibly be, the princess wondered?

A strange idea entered her mind. Perhaps it was because this was a Hebrew child and these were Egyptian nursemaids. Could the infant possibly know the difference? It seemed absurd. And yet, what could the princess do but try? And so, with the aid of Miriam who volunteered her help, a Hebrew nursemaid was found. In fact, without revealing this to the princess, Moses was brought to his own mother, Yocheved, who was hired to *nurse her own child*. God had sent Moses home in order to be nursed from the milk of his very own mother.

Adds the *Midrash*: the mouth that was destined to speak with God could not be profaned by coming in contact with the breasts of idolaters. More, Moses had to imbibe his Jewishness from the life-giving source of his own ancestry.

The Coincidence Surrounding the Day on Which Moses Was Found in the Ark

An ancient tradition tells us that Moses was born prematurely, three months to be exact. His mother was able to hide him for those three months because Egyptians kept careful records from the time Amrom returned to live with his wife, and they checked for a birth only after nine months had passed. At that time, the Egyptians began their search. So on what would have been the "due date," his mother, Yocheved, took Moses and placed him into the ark. The date? The sixth day of *Sivan*, three months after Moses' birthday on the seventh of Adar.

It was on the sixth of Sivan that the life of Moses was saved. It was on the sixth of Sivan that he was found in the ark. And a little over eighty years later, it would be on the sixth of Sivan that the Jewish people gathered around Mount Sinai to receive the Ten Commandments. As Moses had been placed into an ark, so, too, would the tablets of stone proclaiming God's message of ethics and morality to the world find a place in the ark that accompanied the Jews throughout their journeys in the wilderness.

There was an ark for Moses, and there was an ark for the Divine Law. That was God's way of showing that both His messenger and His words deserve the same reverence and protection.

Moses Was Almost Put to Death as a Little Child Because of the Glitter of Gold

The *Midrash* tells how Pharaoh himself was attracted to this beautiful boy adopted by his daughter. One day, while playing with the king, Moses grabbed Pharaoh's crown from off his head and placed it on his own. The magicians of Egypt, as well as the king's advisors, were frightened by what they took to be a terrible omen. Perhaps this was a sign that this child would someday succeed in replacing the Pharaoh.

Some advised death. Others counseled a test: "Surely this was no more than the prank of a child. Let us put before him a gold vessel and a live coal. If he stretches out his hand for the gold, then he has sense and you can slay him. If, however, he reaches for the live coal, then his actions are no more than the antics of a foolish child, and we may be compassionate and spare him."

The plan was approved. They brought gold and burning coal and placed them both before Moses. The child was about to reach for the gold when the angel Gabriel, sent by God for this mission, came and brushed his hand aside, forcing Moses to seize the coal. His hand now aflame, Moses rushed the live coal into his mouth, burning his tongue, with the result that from that day forward Moses became "slow of speech and of tongue."

Moses' lifelong speech impediment was the result of angelic intervention. Had Moses reached for the gold, he would have been slain. Moses' physical defect was something that actually saved his life! Who knows how many of our disabilities are really the saving grace of divine intervention.

The Choice of Profession That Made Moses Worthy of Leading the Jewish People

Starting a new life in Midian, Moses settled down, married, and became a shepherd. Not a menial job at all, explains the *Midrash*. God never gives an exalted office to a person until he has tested him in little things. "Let me see," said the Almighty, "whether his compassion extends even to animals, the beasts of the field. If he can show care toward the lowest creatures, then I will allow him to shepherd my holy flock as well."

Our dealings with those who are mightier than us reflect no more than pragmatic self-interest. Our friendship with equals can also be easily explained as self-serving, doing good to others today in hopes of reciprocity tomorrow. It is only in the way we treat those over whom we rule that we honestly express our true character. That's why kindness to animals is an incomparable barometer of our humanity.

One day, the *Midrash* confides, Moses saw that one of the sheep in his care was unable to walk to the water bank. Moses wept and cried out: "How could I not have realized that you are in need?" He took the sheep and carried it on his shoulders to the water. It was then that the voice of God was heard: "You who have compassion on a flock of animals are worthy of pasturing Israel, my people, for whom I the Lord am their shepherd."

Animals

A righteous man regards the soul of his beast.   —Proverbs

Do not eat before you have fed your animals.   —Talmud

To relieve an animal of pain or danger is a biblical law, superseding any rabbinic ordinance.   —Talmud

Training a child not to step on a caterpillar is as important to the child as it is to the caterpillar.   —Bradley Miller

The behavior of men to lower animals, and their behavior to each other, bears a constant relationship.   —Herbert Spencer

Only animals were not expelled from Paradise.   —Milan Kundera

Let us remember the pets we've had who gave us so much love: _____

_____

_____

_____

_____

_____

_____

What Moses Really Looked Like

History doesn't allow us the benefit of photographic images of our ancient heroes. Yet we all would love to have a mental image of a hero like Moses. What did he look like? Was his saintliness immediately evident on the surface? Did his appearance clearly proclaim his greatness? Were his features more angelic than human?

The *Midrash* describes a moment when these very questions intrigued a non-Jewish contemporary of Moses. The fame of the great Jewish leader had spread afar, reaching a king of Arabia. The king was infatuated with the study of physiognomy. He believed that every man is responsible for his face. Our countenances can be "read." Our characters are plainly revealed by our features.

The inquisitive king sent his finest artist to visit with Moses and to paint his portrait. That would allow him to test his theory and, finally, to see the likeness of a divine human figure. The artist returned after many months to display his work. But the king was aghast. Clearly, the portrait was the image of a villain, a haughty, sensual, immoral person. Surely, the king said, this cannot be the Moses of whom we have heard such great things!

The king was incensed, feeling that an artist who had probably never even personally seen the real Moses misled him. He decided to take the lengthy trip upon himself. With great difficulty, he managed at last to meet the man he was sure would bear the facial image of perfection. But the meeting with Moses shook the king beyond words. Moses indeed looked as he had been painted by the artist!

The king could not hide his disappointment. Surely this spelled the defeat of his long-held belief in the accuracy of physiognomy. Painfully, he shared his feelings with Moses.

The *Midrash* concludes with an ironic O. Henry twist: "No," Moses told the king, "your artist is an expert and your science is quite correct. Indeed, my appearance speaks of my nature and in it you see much evil. That is because I am possessed of many reprehensible traits. I am far from perfect by nature. What I have thankfully been able to accomplish is to master my evil impulses with my strong will. Severe discipline has overcome my innate disposition. If there are those who say I am great, it is not because I was born that way but only because through the hardest of work I have made myself such."

Great people aren't born that way. Greatness isn't a given, it's an achievement. Truth be told, the harder it is for someone to transform himself, the more honored should that person be and the more glorious his accomplishment.

The Idea of the Sabbath Preceded Its Inclusion in the Ten Commandments

Sent by God to return to Egypt and plead with Pharaoh for the freedom of his people, Moses tried many different approaches. Realizing that Pharaoh would truly not agree immediately to "let my people go," Moses thought of an idea that might be acceptable to the Egyptian ruler while easing at least somewhat the burden of slavery.

Making an appointment with the king, Moses suggested that he had a plan that Pharaoh, for reasons of self-interest, could not possibly refuse. "Your goal is to get as much work out of these people as you can. You want them to build pyramids for you and to make your empire prosper. It is an admitted fact that if a slave is not afforded rest at least one day in the week, he will surely die of overexertion. Your slaves will perish unless you allow them one day out of seven to rest from their labors. Give them a Sabbath and it will be for you a source of blessing."

Remarkably, the *Midrash* concludes, the Pharaoh acceded to this request. Years before Sinai, thanks to Moses, Jews enjoyed the blessing of the Sabbath. Much later, God confirmed what Moses intuitively understood. The divine voice decreed the Sabbath day as a time of universal blessing meant not only for slaves to find a weekly respite from their burdens of Torah but for free people of all ages to discover a serenity that will allow for discovering the spiritual meaning to life.

The Sabbath

More than Israel has kept the Sabbath, the Sabbath has kept Israel.
—Ahad HaAm

There is no Judaism without the Sabbath.   —Leo Baeck

The Sabbath is the greatest wonder of religion. Nothing can appear simpler than this institution. Yet no legislator in the world hit on this idea! To the Greeks and Romans it was an object of derision, a superstitious usage. But it removed with one stroke a contrast between slaves who must labor incessantly and their masters who may celebrate continuously.   —Benno Jacob

If Israel observed properly two Sabbaths, they would be redeemed immediately.   —Talmud

Moses Was Almost Killed by God on His Way to Save the Jewish People

The story appears very cryptically in the Bible. "And it was on the road, in an inn, and He (God) sought to slay him (Moses)." What crime could Moses possibly have committed to deserve death? What sin was so great that it deserved such severe punishment?

The angel of death departed from Moses only after Zipporah, his wife, realizes what he had overlooked. They had just had a son eight days before. The child ought to have been circumcised. But Moses did not fulfill this parental duty. For this lapse, Moses deserved to die. Zipporah grabbed a flint and personally performed the *brit milah*, the commandment of circumcision. Then the divine decree was revoked, and Moses was allowed to live.

The *Midrash* is incredulous at this tale. How could Moses possibly have committed the terrible crime of failing to perform the *brit* on his son? How could Moses have rationalized his behavior? The *Midrash* explains by way of a powerful insight: Moses was on the way to fulfilling a historic mission with great meaning for the entire Jewish people. On the way, he was confronted with a familial obligation that would delay him. His own family or his people, he wondered? Which responsibility is greater? Shall I ignore my child because I have to perfect the world? Or shall I put the world on hold while I tend first to my most immediate task as a father?

Moses chose poorly. He had no prior example to guide him. He selected the claim of the crowd over the cry of his own child. His intention was noble but his decision was flawed. God almost killed Moses, so that we, the biblical readers, may never again be tempted to make the same error.

Yes, we all should strive to do our part in changing the world. But the correct sequence for playing our roles in *tikun olan*—improving the world—is to start at the center of our personal universe and then slowly extend our reach outwards to the rest of the world.

First come our own families. That isn't selfish. It's realistic. It's practical. And it's what God Himself commands.

The First Three of the Ten Plagues Against Egypt Were Brought into Motion Not by Moses, but by His Brother Aaron

The first plague was blood. The waters of the Nile turned red, undrinkable, and vivid testimony to the blood shed by the Egyptians as they cast Jewish babies into the Nile. Moses warns Pharaoh and then, in accordance with God's instructions, commands Aaron, his brother to "lift up his rod and to smite the waters that were in the river."

The second plague is a swarm of frogs that covered the land and gave the Egyptians not a moment's peace, as they had done to their Jewish slaves. Here, too, it was Aaron who stretched out his hand over the waters of Egypt, striking them and bringing forth this plague on the land.

One more time, for the plague that followed, God said to Moses, "Say unto Aaron, stretch out your rod and smite the dust of the earth that it may become gnats throughout all the land of Egypt."

Moses was God's messenger. Yet for the first three plagues, it was Aaron who was appointed to strike the ground and the water to bring forth the plagues.

The *Midrash* needs to understand why. It concludes that there is a profound ethical message implicit in this procedure.

Years before Moses had been saved—once by the water and another time by the ground of Egypt. It was the waters of the Nile that carried his basket to safety and salvation. It was the ground that hid the Egyptian that Moses slew while protecting his fellow Hebrew. That is why *Moses could not be the one to strike the very things that had saved him*! Earth and water may be inanimate objects. But the way we deal with the inanimate serves as example of the way we relate to human beings in similar circumstances.

Gratitude is so noble a characteristic that we have to express it even to those completely unaware of our behavior. Gratitude does more for the one who expresses it than the one who receives it.

There Was a Time When God Told the People They Ought to Stop Praying

The Jews had fled from Egypt only to discover that their former slave masters were pursuing them. When they reached the Red Sea, they realized their grave danger. What could they do? And so they began to pray.

Seemingly, they should have been praised for their profession of faith. They lifted their hands to God. What more could they possibly have done? The *Midrash* provides the answer. There is a time for prayer and there is also a time for action. That is what God meant when, in response to the prayers of the Jews at that moment, he proclaimed, "Why do you cry out unto me? Speak unto the children of Israel that they go forward."

Go forward! Move! Act! Do not just lift up your hands to God but raise your hands against your enemies. Do not rely solely on miracles. Indeed, the proverb is a biblical truth: "God helps those who are prepared to help themselves."

Prayer is a program but not a panacea. Prayer is a positive approach when it is merged with the recognition of human responsibility. Pray, the *Midrash* teaches, as if everything depends on God; do as if everything depends on you.

Not Every Single Egyptian Died at the Red Sea— In Fact, There Was One Survivor

The *Midrash* has a tradition that while the entire Egyptian army drowned, their leader escaped. Remarkably enough, Pharaoh survived. The one we would have assumed most worthy of divine retribution and punishment for his evil deeds lived on.

How can anyone make sense of this seemingly skewed application of divine justice? Here again, the *Midrash* provides a brilliant answer.

Of course Pharaoh had to be punished on a far more severe scale than any of his subjects. That's exactly why he was spared! Imagine a ruler without his subjects, a king lacking his kingdom.

Perhaps it can be compared in modern times to the story of the despotic Sadam Hussein whose sons perished but who divine justice condemned to survive, first in a spider hole and then in a solitary cell to spend his remaining days contemplating his fate. Indeed, concludes the *Midrash*, there can be no more severe punishment for a Pharaoh than a life without his crown.

How Moses Chose the People Who Helped Him to Rule the Jews as They Wandered in the Desert

God gave only this instruction to guide Moses: "Choose for me seventy men from among the elders of Israel." They were to become the heads of the Sanhedrin, the highest official Jewish body of law, comparable to the Supreme Court.

But what were the qualifications for assuming this high office? Who was worthy of this great position of leadership alongside of Moses?

The *Midrash* provides the answer. When the Jews were enslaved in Egypt, they were ruled by two different kinds of overseers. The first were Egyptians. They were task masters comparable in modern times to Nazi Gestapo and SS men, sadistic people in power, controlling by way of the whip and the lash. With them, however, were another class of people given a measure of responsibility. They were selected from among the Jews themselves. The intention was similar to what the Nazis achieved with their *kapos*—Jews granted a little bit more food and freedom so they could betray their own people. Many modern-day *kapos* may have done their master's bidding. But in the biblical story, Jewish overseers given the task of ensuring that whip-producing quotas were met, chose to be beaten themselves rather than to inflict harm on their fellow Jews.

These were the people whose heroism was recalled in later years. These were the people worthy of Jewish leadership. Says the *Midrash*: "A Jewish leader is someone who would rather bear the suffering of his people on his own back than to cause pain to others."

These are the three leaders I most admire and the reasons why I respect them:

_____

_____

_____

_____

_____

_____

_____

_____

_____

_____

_____

_____

_____

_____

Some Favorite Things
at the Seder Table

It's So Inspiring to See . . .

The Seder Plate, with its reminders of our miraculous deliverance from the slavery of Egypt. Before us are the very same items that have been part of every Passover celebration since the birth of the Jewish people:

- *Zro'a,* a roasted shank bone of lamb or chicken neck, symbolizing the paschal sacrifice at the Holy Temple in Jerusalem on the afternoon before Passover.
- *Beitza,* a hard-boiled egg, representing the festival sacrifice brought at the Holy Temple.
- *Maror,* bitter herbs or grated fresh horseradish, symbolizing the suffering of the Jews in Egypt.

- *Charoses,* a mixture of finely chopped apples, nuts, and cinnamon moistened with wine made to resemble the mortar used by Israelites to make bricks while enslaved in Egypt.
- *Karpas,* either parsley, celery, or lettuce, to signify that this is a spring holiday.
- *Chazeres,* romaine lettuce (or fresh horseradish), used in the "sandwich" later on in the Seder. It, too, is meant to symbolize the bitterness of oppression by way of an added insight: Romaine lettuce is not bitter to the taste at present; it is only "inherently" bitter, becoming unpleasant at a later time. We must be alert to the bitterness of an enemy even before his cruelty becomes fully apparent!

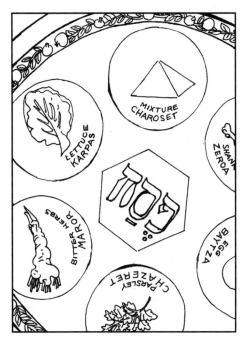

Why do these symbols speak so powerfully to us? Because we know these very same foods have conveyed their messages for centuries to every one of our ancestors, no matter where they lived or what language they spoke. Symbols are universal and eternal. They can communicate far more than speech. They address not our minds but our souls; their medium is not prose but poetry.

Thomas Carlyle understood it well when he wrote: "In a symbol there is concealment and yet revelation: In the symbol, there is ever, more or less distinctly and directly, some embodiment and revelation of the Infinite; the Infinite is made to blend itself with the Finite, to stand visible, and as it were, attainable there. By symbols, accordingly, is man guided and commanded, made happy, made wretched."

Imagine! Because of these symbols, we sit at our Seder and can experience the same feelings as Jews of old, in Poland and Russia, in Persia and Babylonia, in ancient Palestine and in modern-day Israel. They speak in a universal language that transcends time and space. That is why they can so powerfully link us with our past. And that is why these symbols are sacred.

It's So Inspiring to See . . .

The Wine on the Table That We Will Be Pouring for the Traditional "Four Cups" at the Seder

Wine was created, says the Talmud, for two reasons: to comfort mourners in times of tragedy and to permit us to fully rejoice in moments of celebration. It is an anesthetic for our pain and a stimulant for our pleasure. With its capacity to soothe us and to delight us, it is a precious gift from God to the world.

Passover makes us recall both the bad and the good. We were slaves and we were freed. We suffered, but God sent Moses to deliver us. Not once but four times in our history we witnessed God's miraculous intervention.

- First there was Egypt and the exodus. We survived because, as we discovered, God is involved with our history; He cares about our continued existence.
- Next came the return from Babylonian exile. After witnessing the destruction of the First Temple in 586 B.C.E., there were many who were ready to write

off the survival of our people. No other nation had ever been so thoroughly conquered and exiled from its homeland to subsequently return. As the Bible puts it, "By the rivers of Babylon, there we wept." We cried for a past that seemed beyond redemption. Yet again God intervened and a short seventy years later, we returned. That was a second national miracle. It surely deserves drinking a second cup.

❧ That was followed by the miracle of Purim, in the fourth century before the common era, recorded in the book of Esther. In the empire of Persia, Haman, chief advisor to King Achashveros, plotted the first genocide in history. Casting a lottery, "Purim" in Persian, he chose a date in the month of Adar to carry out his plan. He felt it extremely propitious because he discovered that it was the very day on which Moses had died years before. What he did not know was that on that self-same day, Moses was born. Moses' life was complete, so that in fact he left this earth on the same day he was born. With God's intervention, Haman's plan was foiled, and a day of mourning was turned into a day of feasting. The "lottery" became the holiday of Purim, a third vivid reminder of divine intervention for Jewish survival.

❧ Finally, in the second century before the common era, the Maccabees, a small family of priests, overcame the might of the Greek Empire as well as the allure of Hellenic culture that threatened the very existence of the Temple and Jewish freedom of worship. They rededicated the Temple—using a flask of oil for the light of the Menorah that should only have lasted one day but miraculously burnt for eight—and instituted the observance of Hanukkah.

Surely each one of these four miracles deserves a toast to God. We lift our glasses to Him four times at the Seder for every one of these miracles of the past. And then we pour yet a fifth cup for Elijah, the prophet predicted to announce the coming of the Messiah, in order to demonstrate our faith in yet one more miracle—our final redemption.

The Matzah, the Flat Unleavened Bread Commanded as the Special Food for Passover

Why eat matzah? We begin the Seder by explaining it's because "this is the bread of affliction that our ancestors ate in the land of Egypt." Slaves didn't have time to make fully baked bread. Their menu was matzah, the kind of bread that wasn't kept in the oven long enough to rise. Matzah is a symbol of the harshness of our ancestors' lives as slaves.

Yet we're also told that matzah is a symbol of another part of the story. When God took us out of Egypt, the miracle took place literally overnight. We didn't even have time to bake bread for the journey. We grabbed the quickly baked matzahs and rejoiced in our freedom.

So what does the matzah symbolize—our years of forced labor or our unexpectedly speedy deliverance? The answer is both! Because there is a profound truth in one symbol capturing two such dissimilar ideas: *The seed of our freedom was implanted in our servitude*. Only those who have been slaves can truly appreciate freedom.

Why did God make the Jews endure the rigors of Egypt before they came to Sinai? So that, answer the rabbis, throughout history they will be able to empathize with all those who suffer as they did.

Three Matzahs and Four Cups of Wine in Front of Us at the Seder Table

Numbers have special meanings. They bring with them their own unique messages. There's even a section in the Haggadah, (literally *the* telling) the book from which we read at the Seder, that outlines what every number symbolizes:

One stands for God, the Creator of the universe. *Two* are the tablets on which God inscribed the Ten Commandments. *Three* are our patriarchs, the founders of the Jewish religion, Abraham, Isaac, and Jacob. *Four* are our matriarchs, Sarah, Rebecca, Rachel, and Leah, the women who bore, nursed, and nurtured our first families. Small wonder then that some of the most important rituals of the Seder are connected with the numbers three and four:

Three matzahs to remind us that we are descended from three people who personified our highest values. If we learn to live by their ideals, we, too, will deserve to be saved in all times of persecution.

Four cups, four questions asked by our children as part of the Passover ritual, four sons as described in the Haggadah—everything relating to our children and our survival—are linked with our mothers. It is mothers who play the most crucial role in the perpetuation of the Jewish people.

We were saved from Egypt, says the Talmud, "in the merit of the righteous women of that generation." It was because of the strength, the courage, and the goodness of the mothers of that time that God considered the Jews worthy of His intervention. And that, predict the sages, is how we will be deserving of Messiah as well!

Women

A woman of valor who can find? Her price is far above rubies.
　　　　　　　　　　　　　　　　　　—Book of Proverbs 31:10

Everything depends on the Woman.　　—Midrash

If I were asked . . . to what the singular prosperity and growing strength of Americans ought mainly to be attributed, I should reply: To the superiority of their women.　　—Alexis De Tocqueville

Women are the architects of society.　　—Harriet Beecher Stowe

God couldn't be everywhere—so He created mothers.　　—Proverb

These are some of the very special women of our family's past who should always be remembered: _____

_____

_____

_____

_____

_____

_____

_____

The Guests Sitting at the Seder

The very first thing we read in the Haggadah is an invitation for guests to come and join us at the Seder. "Let all who are hungry come in and eat; let all who are needy come and join in our Passover celebration."

Who taught us this great commandment of welcoming strangers to our midst? The Bible tells us that this was the defining trait of Abraham, the very first Jew. No sooner did he circumcise himself than he sat at the door of his tent waiting for passersby to offer them food and lodging. That's what being Jewish meant to him. A religion whose most important commandment is to love one's neighbor as oneself, surely wants us to stress acts of kindness above anything else.

A Seder without guests, say the sages, is like a Sabbath table without the presence of lit candles—dark, depressing, and spiritually barren. Judaism teaches, "The poor does for the host more than the host for the poor." More, the Talmud dares to offer the maxim "Hospitality to wayfarers is even greater than welcoming the Divine Presence." God, after all, doesn't need us; the friendless and homeless, on the other hand, surely do.

Some of the best Seders we've ever had were those we shared with these people:

Some Favorite Passover Rituals

It's So Beautiful When . . .

We do *Bi'ur Chometz*, burning the bread before the start of the holiday. All year long we can't get enough of all the breads that make our mouths salivate. Rye bread, French bread, sourdough, and pumpernickel—they are like manna from heaven. But on the day before Passover, we get together around a fire and burn the last pieces of bread we'll see until the end of the holiday. For eight days, the staple of our normal diet is just as much off-limits as pork, and we won't even permit any small crumbs to remain in our home.

The symbolism is perhaps one of the most important messages in the Bible. Yes, "Man does not live by bread alone." Bread can fill your stomach, but it can't satisfy your soul. Bread is dough, and in almost every culture dough is identified with money. But every once in a while we've got to stop our frantic pursuit of the dollar to remind ourselves that there's more to life than what we own; what's really important is who we *are*. Einstein was a real genius not just because of his theory of relativity. He was smart enough to advise, "Try not to be a man of success; try to become a person of values."

When Jack Benny was given the choice by a mugger, "Your money or your life," the decision was so difficult that Benny is famous for his answer, "I'm thinking, I'm thinking." Are we any smarter? Do we realize that dough is expendable? *Bi'ur Chometz* reminds us that we can live without bread, but we can't live without a spiritual reason for living; without a divine purpose to life, our existence is pointless.

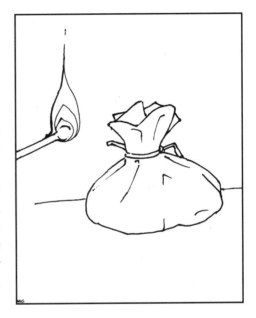

Money

You aren't wealthy until you have something money can't buy.
—Garth Brooks

Prosperity is a way of living and thinking, and not just money or things. Poverty is a way of living and thinking, and not just a lack of money or things.   —Eric Butterworth

Money is just a way to keep score. The best people in any field are motivated by passion.   —Eric S. Raymond

Money never made a man happy yet, nor will it. There is nothing in its nature to produce happiness. The more a man has, the more he wants. Instead of filling a vacuum, it makes one.   —Benjamin Franklin

If money be not thy servant, it will be thy master. The covetous man cannot so properly be said to possess wealth, as that may be said to possess him.   —Francis Bacon

It is good to have money and the things that money can buy, but it's good too, to check up once in a while and make sure you haven't lost the things money can't buy.   —George Lorimer

Who is rich? He who rejoiceth in his portion.   —Talmud

It's So Beautiful When . . .

We Light the Candles to Usher In the Holiday

There is a tradition in many families to light not just two candles but an additional candle for every child in the family as well. Parents explain to their children that every one of them brought extra light to their home when they came into their lives.

The light of a candle, the sages teach, is a symbol of the soul. All things in life that are material obey the law of gravity and fall from above to below. A flame, though, appears to jump up; it constantly strives to rise ever closer to heaven. So too, the spiritual part of our being always struggles to ascend to a higher level. It's never satisfied with where it is; it seeks to come ever closer to perfection.

When our kids tell us that what they admire is everything that is "cool," we remind them, by way of our Sabbath and holiday candles, that the best things in life are the warmth of our love and the fiery passion of our commitments to our family, our people, and our God. And those aren't reserved for the two candles that represent Mom and Dad—there's one for every member of our family because they all do so much to brighten our lives.

Candles

In moments of discouragement, defeat, or even despair, there are always certain things to cling to. Little things usually: remembered laughter, the face of a sleeping child, a tree in the wind—in fact, any reminder of something deeply felt or dearly loved.

No man is so poor as not to have many of these small candles. When they are lighted, darkness goes away—and a touch of wonder remains.
                                           —Tombstone inscription in Britain

Rather light candles than curse the darkness.   —Adlai E. Stevenson

Thousands of candles can be lighted from a single candle, and the life of the candle will not be shortened. Happiness never decreases by being shared.   —Midrash

If you have knowledge, let others light their candles at it.
—Margaret Fuller

A little light will dispel much darkness.   —Midrash

Let us walk in the light of the Lord.   —Isaiah

Lord, may it be Thy will to place us on the side of light.   —Talmud

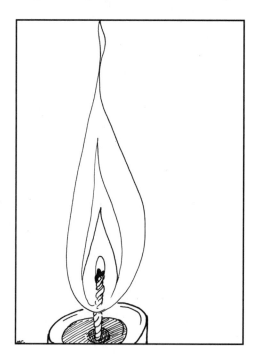

We Dip a Potato into Salt Water

Salt water is a symbol of the tears shed by our ancestors. The Jews in Egypt cried—and they weren't ashamed of their tears. Crying has become unfashionable in our generation. It's looked at as a sign of weakness; "Real men," goes the saying, "don't cry."

Yet the Bible tells us that Jacob wept when Joseph disappeared. David wept when he saw that his beloved son Absalom had died. Jeremiah wept for the destruction of Jerusalem. They all shed tears and weren't ashamed. Tears, says the Talmud, are so powerful that they can break through any gate. Why were the Jews of Egypt saved? Because God heard their weeping.

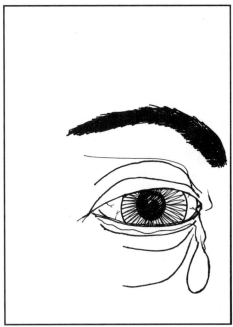

Crying is God's gift to mankind to help us wash away our pains. Tears are shed from our eyes because it is the eyes that have witnessed our sorrows. The first people ever to cry, says the Midrash, were Adam and Eve when they were expelled from Paradise. God stored their tears in the heavens so that from them He could make the rains that bring blessing to earth. It is from the bitter moments of life that we end up deriving unexpected fulfillment.

No life is free from occasional dippings in "salt water." Our prayers should not be never to experience pain; what we should hope for is that our pain always be for a higher purpose.

The times in my life when I cried were when_____

_____

_____

_____

_____

_____

We Sit at the Passover Seder and Lean in Our Seats

Free people, the rabbis explain, lean rather than sit rigidly in their seats. Leaning shows that we are no longer slaves. And that symbolically has a deeper meaning.

Some people are so fixed in their own ideas they can never even listen to another opinion. They are rigid in their mindsets and in their prejudices. They no longer think; they only hold on to the same thoughts they had about everything, be it a year, a decade, or a lifetime ago. They are simply incapable of bending, even a little.

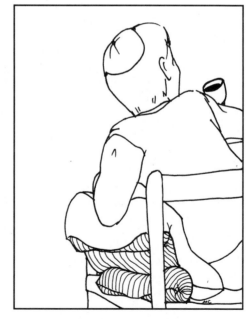

The Seder is a time not just for talking but for discussing and, yes, even debating. Free people have the courage to allow all views a hearing. Free people aren't slaves to others or even to the person they were in their past.

Judaism is thankfully a religion strong enough to tolerate questioning. That's the very theme of the holiday—children asking questions. Let the leader of the Seder lean, says tradition, the better to hear every whisper. Let him be willing to "bend" just a little to tolerate everyone present, even the "wicked son." In that way, the goal of the holiday will be achieved and the Jewish people will survive.

We Eat the Bitter Herbs

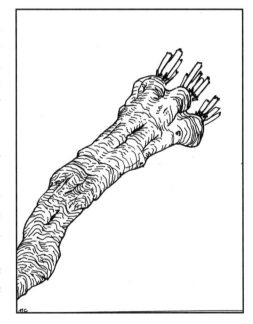

The Chofets Chayim, a revered and saintly rabbi of the early twentieth century, once met a former student and asked him how he was faring. "Oh," the young man replied, "things are bad, very bad indeed."

"God forbid," the rabbi angrily said, "don't ever speak like that. Don't say things are bad, say they are bitter."

"Bad, bitter," the student stammered, "what's the difference? My life is cursed. What does it matter which word I use—it's all the same thing!"

"No, no, not at all," said the Chofets Chayim. "A medicine may be bitter, but it is never bad."

Bitter describes the immediate sensation. Bad is a judgment not only for the present but for the future as well. Our lives often confront us with bitter moments that are not necessarily bad. Faith asks that we allow for the possibility that difficulties are no more than bitter medicines, distasteful but ultimately beneficial. That's why even bitter herbs warrant a blessing.

In my Life, I learned that "Bitter" things aren't necessarily bad when _____

_____

_____

_____

_____

_____

_____

_____

We Eat a Hard-Boiled Egg as a Part of the Seder

What's so special about an egg? An egg has a peculiar characteristic. Most things melt under heat. An egg does the opposite. It becomes hard. And that, Jewish tradition teaches, is the uniqueness of the Jewish people. Instead of disappearing from the pages of history as a result of oppression, Jews became toughened by tragedy, strengthened by affliction.

What a fitting message for Passover! God saved us from Egypt, but why, the rabbis wonder, were we doomed to be slaves there in the first place? Couldn't God in His mercy have spared us the entire experience? The Bible answers the question enigmatically in the book of Deuteronomy. It likens the Egyptian exile to a "fiery furnace of steel." A furnace is used to purify metal so that it becomes better as a result of the refining process. The first exile prepared us for future exiles; years of slavery gave us strength.

Eggs and Jews? Yes, not only because we're so often "eggheads" and bright but also because tough times won't get us down; they'll only make us tougher.

We Spill a Drop of Wine from Our Cup
Every Time We Mention One of the Ten Plagues

Sure, the plagues were an integral part of the story. God punished our enemies for all the evil they inflicted on us. The plagues were necessary—but that doesn't mean we have to rejoice at the suffering of others. What an amazing idea: our cup isn't full, we have to remove a little wine every time we reflect on the fact that our freedom had to come as a result of another's suffering!

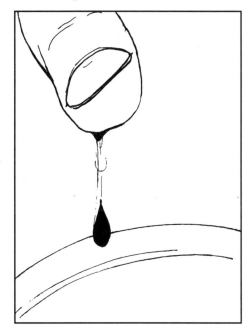

Golda Meir is famous for her equally remarkable observation. "We can forgive the Arabs for almost everything," she said. "We can even forgive them for killing our children. We can never forgive them, though, for turning our children into killers."

The Seder is a time for joy—but we always have to remember what it is we're supposed to be happy about. The Midrash records a fascinating conversation between God and the angels. As the Egyptians were drowning, the angels wanted to burst out in song. After all, wicked people were at last receiving their just punishment. "Stop," said God, "halt your rejoicing. The works of my hands, human beings, are perishing; how dare you use this moment to sing?!"

Our hearts should be big enough to encompass compassion even for those who don't deserve it.

We Make a Sandwich in Imitation of Hillel

Hillel was the first-century sage who combined two pieces of matzah with a bitter-herb filling. What a strange combination! Matzah reminds us of when we left Egypt; bitter herbs remind us of the time when we were there. Aren't they mutually exclusive?

No, Hillel taught, the message of each food becomes enhanced when it is combined with the other. *We can't really appreciate freedom unless we recall the alternative.*

Our grandparents who lived through the Depression truly understood the blessings of prosperity. They never took anything for granted. They didn't believe they were automatically entitled to everything. They knew to thank God for the good things that came their way after enduring deprivation for so many years. Matzah tastes so much better when it comes after bitter herbs.

Kirk Douglas said, "I was able to give my children the blessings of almost everything I never enjoyed. The one thing I haven't been able to give them, though, that has given me so much in life is the poverty of my childhood." The least we can do, now that we are no longer slaves, is to "sandwich" into our good times some of the taste of the bad.

Prosperity

Prosperity is the surest breeder of insolence I know.   —Mark Twain

If we had no winter, the spring would not be so pleasant: if we did not sometimes taste of adversity, prosperity would not be so welcome.
—Anne Bradstreet

When prosperity comes, do not use all of it.   —Confucius

Prosperity discovers vice, adversity discovers virtue.   —Francis Bacon

Everything in the world may be endured, except continual prosperity.
—Goethe

The Children Return the Afikomen in Exchange for a Present

The custom is ancient: The head of the household wraps a small piece of matzah at the very beginning of the Seder to be used as the "Afikomen"—the "dessert" of a last bite of matzah meant to linger as the final memory of the Passover meal. Since it will be needed, it's "hidden"—but purposely not very well. The youngest child is encouraged to find it and told that if successful will be rewarded with a gift of his or her choosing. A game of hide-and-seek is built into the solemn spirituality of a Seder!

Religion is often mistakenly thought to demand a life of sacrifice and severity. That could not be further from the truth. In Deuteronomy, the Torah lists a string of curses that will befall the Jewish people—and says that these punishments will come "because you did not serve the Lord with joy." Judaism is not ascetic; the smile rather than the frown is the more apt expression of piety.

Whatever God created, He immediately pronounced good. That's why the Talmud teaches that in the world to come we will all be greeted with this remarkable question by the divine interrogator: "Are there any things that God created on earth for mankind to enjoy that you never took advantage of?"

When we teach our children to carry on our beliefs, we need to do it in a way that makes them love our tradition more than to fear divine punishment. Rewards are more powerful educational tools than threats. For that reason, there is a beautiful custom to teach children the *Alef Bet*, the Hebrew alphabet, by placing honey on a plate in the shape of the letters and urging them to lick off the sweet forms.

Bring us the matzah, we say to our little ones, and you will get a wonderful gift. That will remain true for the rest of your lives as well. By observing the beautiful ceremonies of our faith, we promise them they will forever be granted gifts from Above just as they are granted our presents now.

Some of the gifts I've given my children in the past are _____

_____

_____

_____

_____

_____

_____

_____

Gifts

You can give without loving, but you cannot love without giving.
—Amy Carmichael

Let the season of giving be yours and not that of your inheritors.
—Kahlil Gibran

The sick you ask; the well, you give.   —Jewish proverb

Giving to others is getting much for yourself.   —Talmud

It is far better to make sure that your children love you than that they fear you. —Talmud

We Open the Door for Elijah

Why Elijah? Because in Jewish tradition Elijah is the prophet who will announce the coming of the Messiah. And why do we expect him on Passover? Because that's when God first redeemed the Jewish people—so that makes it a good time for Him to bring about the ultimate redemption for all of mankind.

Just imagine, for thousands of years Jews keep expecting a visitor who never comes. Yet we faithfully pour his cup of wine just in case this is the year he is finally going to make an appearance—and even throw open the door in greeting!

What does that say about our sense of reality? Will we never learn to accept no for an answer? Not if God made a promise. We are still the eternal optimists. So what if Elijah is late. That doesn't mean he won't eventually show.

What a message to transmit to our children at the Seder! Disappointments don't deter us from preserving our hopes. Listen for the footsteps of Messiah, we teach the next generation, even if we weren't privileged to welcome him yet. Faith in God and trust in His promises go hand in hand. Someday, maybe *this* very Passover, we'll open the door and be able to welcome a long awaited prophet.

Optimism

Passover must always coincide with the spring season because both represent the spirit of hope and of optimism.   —Midrash

An optimist is the human personification of spring.
—Susan J. Bissonette

Optimism doesn't wait on facts. It deals with prospects.
—Norman Cousins

To the question whether I am a pessimist or an optimist, I answer that my knowledge is pessimistic, but my willing and hoping are optimistic.
—Albert Schweitzer

These are some of the reasons why I want my children to be optimistic about the future:_____

_____

_____

_____

_____

_____

_____

Our Whole Family Joins in Singing the Songs at the Seder

So many melodies bring back precious memories. I love it when we do the refrains for *Dayenu*, and we list all the things that God did for us, every one of which would have been enough to warrant our everlasting thanks. I still get goose bumps when my children, from the youngest—now fully grown—to the oldest ask the four questions to the very same tune I used when I was little. We all take turns for the "Who knows one? Who knows two?" riddle song that concludes the Seder—the one that tests our ability to remember the biblical significance of the numbers one through thirteen— and laugh along as we try to keep our place even while we're fighting sleep and the effects of the wine at the end of the evening.

The songs stir something in us far deeper than mere words can reach. When the Red Sea miraculously parted, they didn't recite a speech, they burst out in song. Song comes from the soul and brings up emotions that would otherwise find no means of expression. If the whole Bible is holy, says the Talmud, then the Song of Songs is the holy of holies.

The song at the shore of the Red Sea begins with the words, "Then will sing Moses and the children of Israel." Not "sang," but "*will* sing." The rabbis explain that this is not only a description of a past event but also a prophecy. Jews *will* sing in the future, in all times when they celebrate this day as well as when they will greet the Messiah. So we sing at our Seder, and we keep creating the memories that ensure our survival.

My favorite Passover songs are: _____

_____

_____

_____

_____

_____

_____

_____

_____

_____

_____

Some Favorite Passover Songs

It's So Moving to Sing Together . . .

Traditional Songs Like . . .

THE FOUR QUESTIONS—MA NISHTANA

Ma nishtana, ha'layla haze
Mikol ha'leylot, mikol ha'leylot

Shebechol ha'leylot anu ochlin,
Hametz u matzah, hametz u matzah
Ha'layla haze, ha'layla haze, kulo matzah
Ha'layla haze, ha'layla haze, kulo matzah

Shebechol ha'leylot anu ochlin,
Shear yerakot, shear yerakot
Ha'layla haze, ha'layla haze, marror, marror
Ha'layla haze, ha'layla haze, marror, marror

Shebechol ha'leylot ein anu matbilin
Afilu pa'am achat, afilu pa'am achat
Ha'layla haze, ha'layla haze, shetei pe'amim
Ha'layla haze, ha'layla haze, shetei pe'amim

Shebechol ha'leylot anu ochlin,
Bein yoshvin u'bein mesubin
Ha'layla haze, ha'layla haze, kulanu mesubin
Ha'layla haze, ha'layla haze, kulanu mesubin

Why is this night different from all other nights?
On all other nights, we eat bread or matzah,
But on this night only matzah.
On all other nights, we eat other greens,
But on this night a bitter vegetable
On all other nights, we do not dip even once,
But on this night we must dip two times.
On all other nights, we eat sitting or leaning,
But on this night we all lean.

DAYENU (IT WOULD HAVE BEEN ENOUGH)

Ilu hotzi, hotzi anu
Hotzi anu mi mitzrayim
Mi mitzrayim, hotzi anu
Dayenu!

If He would have taken us out, taken us out
Taken us out of Egypt
Out of Egypt taken us out
It would have been enough!

Refrain:
Da-dayenu, da-dayenu, da-dayenu
Dayenu, dayenu, dayenu
Da-dayenu, da-dayenu, da-dayenu
Dayenu, dayenu

Ilu natan, natan lanu
Natan lanu torah tovah
Torah tovah, natan lanu
Dayenu!

If He would have given, have given us
Given us a good Torah
A good Torah given to us
It would have been enough!

Ilu natan, natan lanu
Natan lanu et haShabbat
Et haShabbat, natan lanu
Dayenu!

If He would have given, given to us
Given to us the Shabbat
The Shabbat, He would have given to us
It would have been enough!

Eliahu Hanavi (Elijah the Prophet)

Eliahu hanavi
Eliahu hatishbi
Eliahu, Eliahu
Eliahu hagiladi

Elijah the prophet
Elijah the the man from Tishbi
Elijah, Elijah
Elijah the man from Gilead

Bimherah v'yamenu yavo elenu
Im mashiach ben David,
Im mashiach ben David

Speedily and in our days
Together with Messiah the son of David
Together with Messiah the son of David

Eliahu hanavi
Eliahu hatishbi
Eliahu, Eliahu
Eliahu hagiladi

Elijah the prophet
Elijah the the man from Tishbi
Elijah, Elijah
Elijah the man from Gilead

Some Newer Versions of Some of the Traditional Songs Like . . .

ECHAD MI YODAYA (WHO KNOWS ONE?)

Oo Ee Oo Ah Ah. I said Oo Ee Oo Ah Ah.
Who knows one? I know one!
One is haShem, one is haShem, one is haShem,
In the heavens and on earth.

Oo Ee Oo Ah Ah. I said Oo Ee Oo Ah Ah.
Who knows two? I know two!
Two are the tablets that Moshe brought,
And one is haShem, one is haShem, one is haShem,
In the heavens and on earth.

Oo Ee Oo Ah Ah. I said Oo Ee Oo Ah Ah.
Who knows three? I know three!
Three are the Papas,
Two are the tablets that Moshe brought,
And one is haShem, one is haShem, one is haShem,
In the heavens and on earth.

Oo Ee Oo Ah Ah. I said Oo Ee Oo Ah Ah.
Who knows four? I know four!
Four are the Mamas, three are the Papas,
Two are the tablets that Moshe brought,
And one is haShem, one is haShem, one is haShem,
In the heavens and on earth.

Oo Ee Oo Ah Ah. I said Oo Ee Oo Ah Ah.
Who knows five? I know five!
Five are the books of the Torah,
Four are the Mamas, three are the Papas,
Two are the tablets that Moshe brought,
And one is haShem, one is haShem, one is haShem,
In the heavens and on earth.

Oo Ee Oo Ah Ah. I said Oo Ee Oo Ah Ah.
Who knows six? I know six!
Six are the parts of the Mishnah,
Five are the books of the Torah,
Four are the Mamas, three are the Papas,
Two are the tablets that Moshe brought,
And one is haShem, one is haShem, one is haShem,
In the heavens and on earth.

Oo Ee Oo Ah Ah. I said Oo Ee Oo Ah Ah.
Who knows seven? I know seven!
Seven are the days of the week,
Six are the parts of the Mishnah,
Five are the books of the Torah,
Four are the Mamas, three are the Papas,
Two are the tablets that Moshe brought,
And one is haShem, one is haShem, one is haShem,
In the heavens and on earth.

Oo Ee Oo Ah Ah. I said Oo Ee Oo Ah Ah.
Who knows eight? I know eight!
Eight are the days until a bris,
Seven are the days of the week,
Six are the parts of the Mishnah,
Five are the books of the Torah,
Four are the Mamas, three are the Papas,
Two are the tablets that Moshe brought,

And one is haShem, one is haShem, one is haShem,
In the heavens and on earth.

Oo Ee Oo Ah Ah. I said Oo Ee Oo Ah Ah.
Who knows nine? I know nine!
Nine are the months before a baby is born,
Eight are the days until a bris,
Seven are the days of the week,
Six are the parts of the Mishnah,
Five are the books of the Torah,
Four are the Mamas, three are the Papas,
Two are the tablets that Moshe brought,
And one is haShem, one is haShem, one is haShem,
In the heavens and on earth.

Oo Ee Oo Ah Ah. I said Oo Ee Oo Ah Ah.
Who knows ten? I know ten!
Ten are the ten commandments,
Nine are the months before a baby is born,
Eight are the days until a bris,
Seven are the days of the week,
Six are the parts of the Mishnah,
Five are the books of the Torah,
Four are the Mamas, three are the Papas,
Two are the tablets that Moshe brought,
And one is haShem, one is haShem, one is haShem,
In the heavens and on earth.

Oo Ee Oo Ah Ah. I said Oo Ee Oo Ah Ah.
Who knows eleven? I know eleven!
Eleven are the stars in Yosef's dream,
Ten are the ten commandments,
Nine are the months before a baby is born,
Eight are the days until a bris,
Seven are the days of the week,
Six are the parts of the Mishnah,
Five are the books of the Torah,
Four are the Mamas, three are the Papas,
Two are the tablets that Moshe brought,
And one is haShem, one is haShem, one is haShem,
In the heavens and on earth.

Oo Ee Oo Ah Ah. I said Oo Ee Oo Ah Ah.
Who knows twelve? I know twelve!
Twelve are the tribes of yisroel,
Eleven are the stars in Yosef's dream,
Ten are the ten commandments,
Nine are the months before a baby is born,
Eight are the days until a bris,
Seven are the days of the week,
Six are the parts of the Mishnah,
Five are the books of the Torah,
Four are the Mamas, three are the Papas,
Two are the tablets that Moshe brought,

And one is haShem, one is haShem, one is haShem,
In the heavens and on earth.

Oo Ee Oo Ah Ah. I said Oo Ee Oo Ah Ah.
Who knows thirteen? I know thirteen!
Thirteen attributes has haShem,
Twelve are the tribes of yisroel,
Eleven are the stars in Yosef's dream,
Ten are the ten commandments,
Nine are the months before a baby is born,
Eight are the days until a bris,
Seven are the days of the week,
Six are the parts of the Mishnah,
Five are the books of the Torah,
Four are the Mamas, three are the Papas,
Two are the tablets that Moshe brought,
And one is haShem, one is haShem, one is haShem,
In the heavens and on earth.

Some Newer Songs Made Especially for the Children Like . . .

MAKE A MATZAH

Make a matzah, pat, pat, pat
Do not make it fat, fat, fat
Make the matzah nice and flat
Bake the matzah just like that

Make charoset, chop, chop, chop
Apples, nuts, and cinnamon
Add some wine, it's lots of fun!
Make charoset, yum, yum, yum

Some Newer Songs That Tell the Story in English Like . . .

LET MY PEOPLE GO

When Israel was in Egypt's land,
Let my people go!
Oppressed so hard they could not stand,
Let my people go!

Refrain:
Go down, Moses,
Way down in Egypt land
Tell ol' Pharaoh
Let my people go!

Thus saith the Lord, bold Moses said,
Let my people go!
If not, I'll smite your people dead,
Let my people go!

As Israel stood by the water side,
Let my people go!
By G-d's command it did divide,
Let my people go!

Some Newer Songs to Tunes Everyone Knows

Like this one sung to the tune of "My Favorite Things" . . .

Cleaning and cooking and so many dishes
Out with the hametz, no pasta, no knishes
Fish that's gefilted, horseradish that stings
These are a few of our Passover things.

Matzah and karpas and chopped up haroset
Shankbones and Kiddish and Yiddish neuroses
Tante who kvetches and uncle who sings
These are a few of our Passover things.

Motzi and maror and trouble with Pharaohs
Famines and locusts and slaves with wheelbarrows
Matzah balls floating and eggshell's that cling
These are a few of our Passover things.

When the plagues strike
When the lice bite
When we're feeling sad
We simply remember our Passover things
And then we don't feel so bad.

Or like this one sung to the tune of "Take Me Out to the Ballgame!" . . .

Take me out to the Seder
Take me out with the crowd.
Feed me on matzah and chicken legs,
I don't care for the hard-boiled eggs.
And its root, root, root for Elijah
That he will soon reappear.
And let's hope, hope, hope that we'll meet
Once again next year!

Take me out to the Seder
Take me out with the crowd.
Read the Haggadah
And don't skip a word.
Please hold your talking,
We want to be heard.
And lets, root, root, root for the leader
That he will finish his spiel

So we can nosh, nosh, nosh and by-gosh
Let's eat the meal!!!

Or like this one sung to the tune of "I've Been Working on the Railroad" . . .

We've been working on these buildings;
Pharaoh doesn't pay.
We've been doing what he tells us
Mixing straw with clay.
Can't you hear the master calling,
"Hurry up, make that brick!"
Can't you feel the master whip us,
'Til we're feeling sick.

Oy vay, it's a mess,
A terrible distress,
Oy vay, it's a mess for Jews, us Jews.

Moshe's in the palace with Pharaoh,
Warning of all God's clout, clout, clout.
Moshe's in the palace with Pharaoh,
And God's gonna get us out!

We're singing . . .
Fee, Fi, Fiddely eye oh,

Make our matzahs "to go" oh oh oh.
Fee, Fi, Fiddely eye oh,
Stick it to the ol' Pharaoh!

Or like this one sung to the tune of "Maria," from *West Side Story* . . .

Elijah!
I just saw the prophet Elijah.
And suddenly that name
Will never sound the same to me.
Elijah!
He came to our Seder
Elijah!
He had his cup of wine,
But could not stay to dine
This year—
Elijah!
For your message all Jews are waiting:
That the time's come for peace
and not hating—
Elijah—
Next year we'll be waiting.
Elijah!

Or like this one sung to the tune of "Do You Hear the People Sing,"
from *Les Misèrables* . . .

> Do you hear the doorbell ring,
> And it's a little after ten?
> It can only be Elijah
> Come to take a sip again.
> He is feeling pretty fine
> But in his head a screw is loose.
> So perhaps instead of wine
> We should only give him juice.

Or like this one sung to the tune of "Clementine" . . .

THE BALLAD OF THE FOUR SONS

> Said the father to his children,
> "At the Seder you will dine,
> You will eat your fill of matzah,
> You will drink four cups of wine."
>
> Now this father had no daughters,
> But his sons they numbered four.
> One was wise and one was wicked,
> One was simple and a bore.

And the fourth was sweet and winsome,
he was young and he was small.
While his brothers asked the questions
he could scarcely speak at all.
Said the wise one to his father,
"Would you please explain the laws?
Of the customs of the Seder
Will you please explain the cause?"

And the father proudly answered,
"As our fathers ate in speed,
Ate the paschal lamb 'ere midnight
And from slavery were freed."

So we follow their example,
And 'ere midnight must complete
All the Seder and we should not
After twelve remain to eat.
Then did sneer the son so wicked,
"What does all this mean to you?"
And the father's voice was bitter
As his grief and anger grew.

"If you yourself don't consider
You as son of Israel,
Then for you this has no meaning
You could be a slave as well."

Then the simple son said simply,
"What is this," and quietly,
The good father told his offspring
"We were freed from slavery."

But the youngest son was silent,
For he could not ask at all.
His bright eyes were bright with wonder,
As his father told him all.
My dear children, heed the lesson,
and remember evermore,
What the father told his children,
Told his sons that numbered four.

The songs I remember most from my childhood are: _____

_____

_____

_____

_____

_____

_____

_____

_____

_____

Some Favorite Passover Foods

From Appetizer to Compote...

Anticipation

A note of caution before you read the mouthwatering recipes on the pages that follow.

Please Wait

Yes, that's what you really should be sure to do before making these recipes. You see, there's a remarkable rule in the Talmud about Passover food. It's phrased in a way that is almost shocking. The rabbis used a metaphor that we might consider erotic: Anyone who eats matzah on the eve of Passover (the day before the festival begins) is like one who has sexual relations with his bride-to-be in his father-in-law's home.

What they meant is obvious. Waiting for something special increases the joy of fulfillment. Sex before marriage considerably diminishes the excitement of the wedding night. So too, looking forward to the Seder and its special foods brings with it a special sense of delight when we finally taste its offerings. Eat the matzah before the Seder, and you've lost a large part of the Passover experience.

That's why I recommend that some dishes be saved as "holiday treats." They should become associated in our minds—and our stomachs—with special moments. Build up the anticipation. Let the whole family say, "We can't wait for Passover so we can have our favorite . . . ."

Food can be Pavlovian; it can trigger automatic responses. Just thinking about it can make your mouth water; better yet, food can also overwhelm you with memories.

Food

No scholar should live in a town where good food is unavailable.
—Talmud

Eat nothing that will prevent you from eating.
—Last will and testament of Ibn Tibbon

Whoever eats disagreeable food violates three prohibitions: he hurts his health, he wastes food, and he offers a benediction in vain.
—Rabbi Akiba

Friendships develop over food and wine.   —Midrash

The preservation of custom is not an anthropological imperative. It is a moral imperative. My parents taught me this. With these particulars, we prove that we are alive and that we are free. When, on the eve of Passover, I chop apples and walnuts and cinnamon with wine precisely as my parents and their parents chopped them, I mark the defeat of our enemies. In our kitchen, empires fall again.   —Leon Wieseltier

A Seder Essential: *Charoset*

I know it's supposed to remind us of the mortar and the bricks we had to make as slaves, but that doesn't mean it can't also be delicious.

THE EASY WAY TO MAKE IT

    2 cups chopped apples   2 teaspoons cinnamon

    2 cups chopped walnuts   2 tablespoons sweet red wine

Combine and refrigerate.

THE WAY THEY MAKE IT IN JERUSALEM

    ½ cup dates, chopped   ¼ teaspoon ginger

    1 cup chopped apples   1 teaspoon cinnamon

    ½ cup chopped walnuts   1–2 tablespoons sweet red wine

    ½ cup chopped almonds

Combine and refrigerate.

The Opening Act: Tomato Basil Gefilte Fish

Know why Sabbath and holiday meals in Jewish tradition start with fish? It's because they are a fertility symbol—and "gefilte," the Yiddish word for "stuffed," makes the allusion even clearer. Having children is the very first commandment in the Bible: "Be fruitful and multiply." So start your meal traditionally with a gefilte fish that is sure to inflame your appetite as well as your libido.

2 ounces sun-dried tomatoes
2 tablespoons olive oil
8 large onions, peeled and sliced
2 logs frozen gefilte fish
   (preferably Ungars)

1 8-ounce bottle tomato basil
   salad dressing

Preheat oven to 350° degrees F. Rehydrate sun-dried tomatoes by covering with boiling water. Set aside. Heat olive oil and gently sauté onions until translucent, about 10 minutes. Spoon about half the onions into the bottom of 2 loaf pans. Unwrap the fish loaves and place 1 in each pan. Add ½ a bottle of dressing to each pan. Apply tomatoes decoratively to the top of each loaf. Spoon remaining onions into pans on the sides of the loaves. Cook for ½ hour. Cover with foil and cook for another ½ hour. Cool and keep refrigerated. Serve at room temperature.

Makes 16–20 servings.

NEW AND IMPROVED GEFILTE FISH

1 large jar gefilte fish (choose
   your favorite brand)
1 bunch beets
1 bunch carrots

2 large onions
Pepper—lots of it
Salt to taste

1. Take a large jar (8 to 12 pieces).
2. Slice the carrots, beets, and onions. Layer in a heavy stock pot, the beets, pieces of fish, onions, carrots, and seasonings; repeat as many times as is necessary with everything but the beets.

3. Pour the liquid from the jar over the fish, and then bring to a boil. Turn down and simmer for about 45 minutes. Cool, remove from liquid, and serve.

Makes 8–10 servings.

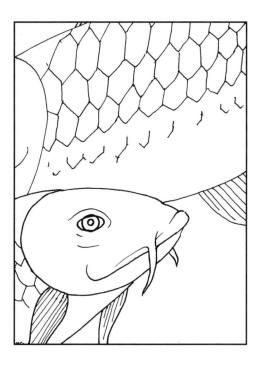

Rich Chicken Soup: Fit for the Seder

Chicken soup, it's long been said, is "Jewish penicillin." Not so strange that doctors are at last coming round to the medical benefits of this traditional holiday favorite. Try this recipe, and you have a good chance, as the blessing goes, "to live to a hundred and twenty."

4–5 pound chicken	2 teaspoons white pepper
3 quarts cold water	1 bay leaf
1 cup carrots, cut into chunks	Salt to taste
4 celery ribs	Few sprigs fresh dill
2 onions, quartered	1 turnip
4 cloves of garlic	1 parsnip

1. Rinse chicken thoroughly.
2. Cut the chicken into 2 or 4 pieces depending on the size of the pot.
3. Cover with water, and bring to a boil.
4. Add vegetables and seasonings.
5. Simmer for 4 hours, skimming occasionally.
6. Strain the soup and cool. Refrigerate until the fat rises to the top and can be separated from the stock.
7. When ready to serve, simmer again (add knaidlech/matzah balls if desired), and heat for 15 or 20 minutes.

Makes 10–11 servings.

Mother's Matzah Balls

Chicken soup without matzah balls? As unthinkable as Jews without God, love without marriage—oh, you get the idea!

4 eggs	4 tablespoons water or
4 tablespoons oil	chicken soup
1 teaspoon salt	1 cup matzah meal

1. Mix first 4 ingredients; then fold in the matzah meal.
2. Refrigerate the batter for about 1 hour, or until batter is thick enough to form balls.
3. Wet hands to form the balls; drop the balls carefully into 2 quarts of boiling salted water or hot soup.
4. Cover and cook for at least 1 hour.
5. Add Matzah Balls to soup.

Makes 12–16 servings.

Elaine's Meat Borsht

Elaine, of course, is my wife. Yes, I know I'm prejudiced because it's one of my wife's specialties. But trust me, you haven't tasted real borsht until you've tried this version.

3 quarts water	1–2 pounds flanken
8 beets	2 onions, sliced
(1 bottle of prepared Borscht	8 cloves of garlic
may be substituted for some	1 tablespoon salt
of the water and the beets)	¼ cup brown sugar
Meat bones	1 teaspoon sour salt

Combine, cook until meat is tender.

Makes 12–14 servings.

The Incredible Passover "Rolls"

Yes, they're Kosher for Passover. What makes a Passover menu so difficult is that we're restricted by way of forbidden ingredients. All leavened products are traditionally off-limits. For years, I missed eating rolls and breads most of all on this holiday. At last I've found a great substitute. I know you'll love it almost as much as "the real thing."

2 cups matzah meal	1 cup water
1 teaspoon salt	½ cup peanut oil
1 tablespoon sugar	4 eggs

1. Combine matzah meal with salt and sugar.
2. Bring oil and water to a boil. Add to matzah meal mixture and mix well.
3. Beat in eggs thoroughly, one at a time.
4. Allow to stand 15 minutes.
5. Oil hands; then shape into rolls, and place on a well-greased cookie sheet
6. Bake in a moderate oven—375°F—for 50 minutes or until golden brown.

Makes 12 servings.

Yummy Orange-Broiled Duck

Ducks come from the water. We crossed the Red Sea as part of the miracle of Passover. So, yes, there's even something symbolic about this choice of a main meal. But more than anything else, this is just an incredibly delicious way to add joy to a holiday meal.

**1 large duck cut in halves
   or quarters
6 tablespoons orange
   marmalade**

**¼ cup sauterne wine
¼ teaspoon ginger**

1. Place duck, skin side down, in a broiler pan with a rack, with top surface 6 inches from the heat.
2. Broil 40–50 minutes, turning several times for even browning. If some spots start to brown too quickly, cover them with aluminum foil.
3. Combine marmalade, wine, and ginger.

4. Brush one side of duck with sauce during last 10 minutes of broiling.

5. Broil 5 minutes.

6. Turn, brush with sauce; broil 5 minutes more.

Makes 2–4 servings.

Elaine's Apricot Roast

I don't know what the paschal lamb the Jews ate at the first Seder meal tasted like—but I'm sure it couldn't have been more mouth-watering than this.

4-pound brisket	½ teaspoon pepper
1½ cup water	2 tablespoons cinnamon
1½ cup brown sugar	½ teaspoon allspice
¼ cup vinegar or lemon juice	½ teaspoon ginger
2 teaspoons salt	

Cook covered at 350°F for 2 hours.
Then add:

½ pound dried apricots
½ pound dried prunes

Recover and cook for 1 more hour; then uncover and cook for an additional hour.

Makes 10–12 servings.

Delicious Stuff-Yourself Stuffing

Use with your favorite chicken or turkey recipe. A Seder meal should be "filling"—both spiritually and physically. Forget about diets for this night, and stuff yourself to your heart's content. You can always say you meant it to be a religious experience!

¾ cup oil	¼ teaspoon pepper
¾ cup minced onion	1 tablespoon paprika
10 matzahs finely broken	1 egg
1 teaspoon salt	2 cups chicken soup

1. Sauté onions in oil until tender but not browned.
2. Add broken matzahs and toast lightly.
3. Combine seasonings, egg, and soup. Add to matzah mixture.
4. Can be cooked either stuffed inside chicken or turkey or cooked in a pan alongside chicken or turkey and basted several times with gravy from the bird.

Makes 10–12 servings.

The "24 Karat" Carrot Kugel

What's a Kugel? Webster's *says it comes from the Yiddish and means "a baked pudding (as of potatoes or noodles) usually served as a side dish." My mother said it's a main dish disguised as a side so as not to embarrass everything else that dares to be on the same plate. You decide after you taste this scrumptious recipe.*

4 ounces margarine	1 pound carrots, grated
½ cup matzah meal	½ cup sugar
1 teaspoon kosher for Passover baking powder	1 teaspoon lemon juice
3 tablespoons potato starch	1 teaspoon cinnamon
½ cup sweet red wine	1 egg, beaten
	Grated lemon rind (optional)

1. Preheat oven to 350°F.
2. Grease 9-inch baking pan. Cream together margarine and matzah meal.
3. Add baking powder and blend. Dissolve potato starch in wine.
4. Combine all ingredients thoroughly.
5. Pour into prepared pan, and bake for 1 hour.

Makes 12–16 servings.

Broccoli-Blessed Knishes

Knish, as a word, comes from Yiddish by way of Polish. Knish as a food probably comes from the Garden of Eden. Where else could something so delectable have had its creation?!

1 cup mashed potatoes	½ teaspoon black pepper
⅓ cup matzah meal	¼ teaspoon salt
2 tablespoons potato starch	1 cup fresh or frozen broccoli,
½ small onion, finely chopped	steamed and finely chopped
2 egg whites	Cooking spray

Preheat oven to 375°F.

Combine, in a bowl, the potatoes, matzah meal, potato starch, onion, egg whites, pepper, and salt and knead together. Divide the dough into six balls and flatten each. Divide the broccoli evenly onto each circle, fold over, and press edges to seal.

Coat a baking sheet generously with the cooking spray. Arrange the knishes in a single layer, and place the baking sheet on the bottom rack of the oven. Bake for 15 minutes on each side. Serve hot.

Makes 6 servings.

Super Bonus: Only 82 calories, no fat

"M.O.M.": Mushroom Onion Matzah Kugel

If I dared to preface it with the letters for MOM, you know it has to be not just good but great!

3 cups matzah farfel or broken matzahs	1 lb. mushrooms
2 large onions	4 eggs
	2 tablespoons oil

Following ingredients to taste:

Salt	Garlic powder
Pepper	

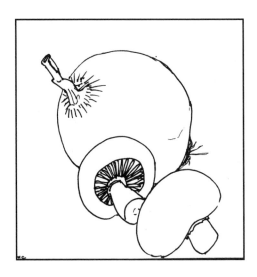

1. Wet farfel in colander with boiling water.
2. Sauté onions and mushrooms then mix with other ingredients; finally, mix with farfel or broken matzahs.
3. Bake in a well-greased pan for 1 hour at 350°F.

Makes 8 servings.

Variety Vegetable Garden Kugel

You didn't think one Kugel alone would do it, did you?

3 stalks celery, sliced	3 tablespoons matzah
4 carrots, sliced	meal
3 medium potatoes, sliced	4 eggs
2 onions, sliced	1 teaspoon salt
2 red peppers	¼ teaspoon pepper
8 ounces mushrooms, sliced	1 tablespoon olive oil

1. Place vegetables on cookie sheet; drizzle olive oil on top.
2. Set oven to broil; put oven rack on highest level.
3. Broil 7 minutes on a side; turn until brown and soft.
4. Add eggs, matzah meal, salt, and pepper.
5. Mix.
6. Bake in sprayed pan for 1 hour at 350°F.

Makes 6 servings.

Dessert at Last: Grandma Gittel's
Nut Torte Supreme

Gittel is my mother of blessed memory. She was a culinary genius, and our whole family treasures this torte in particular.

The biblical miracle was that we survived in the desert. The modern-day miracle is that we survive our desserts. Sure it's too much after such a big meal. But who can resist? And on a holiday, it's actually a religious commandment to rejoice. How better to fulfill that obligation than with these guaranteed perfect endings:

8 eggs separated

8 ounces sugar

7 ounces ground filberts

1 tablespoon Crisco

½ package chocolate chips, ground

1 teaspoon lemon juice

1. Beat ½ cup sugar in egg yolks; add lemon juice.
2. Mix nuts in yolks.
3. Beat ½ cup sugar in egg whites until stiff.
4. Fold nut mixture into egg whites slowly.
5. Bake at 350°F between 45–60 minutes.

Makes 12 servings.

Not-to-Be-Trifled-With Chocolate
Almond Truffles

1 cup (6 ounces) shelled
   almonds
¼ pound semisweet chocolate,
   broken into small pieces
½ cup sugar

2 egg yolks (save egg whites)
1¼ tablespoons dark rum
3 tablespoons unsweetened
   cocoa powder

1. Preheat oven to 350°F; toast almonds in one layer in a shallow baking pan for 15 minutes, stirring occasionally. Allow to cool.
2. Place almonds, chocolate, and sugar in a food processor, and coarsely chop. Add yolks and rum; continue processing until mixture is fine. Test by rolling into a ball; if too dry, add a few drops of the saved egg whites, and process a bit longer.
3. Spread cocoa on a sheet of wax paper.
4. Roll level teaspoonfuls of chocolate-almond mixture into balls in the palm of your hand; then roll in cocoa to coat well.

To improve the taste: These truffles have an extra bonus—they get better with time. Refrigerate and keep enjoying more and more.

Makes 12–16 servings.

The Chocoholic's "I've Gone to Heaven" Chocolate Cream Dessert

1 7-ounce bittersweet chocolate
½ cup sugar

4 eggs, separated
¼ cup strong coffee

1. Melt chocolate in top of double boiler.
2. Add sugar; when smooth, add egg yolks and coffee.
3. Beat egg whites until stiff. Fold into chocolate mixture.
4. Refrigerate until ready to serve.

Can be served in a mold, in parfait dishes, or in a pre-baked pie crust. Add chopped nuts for variety.

Makes 8–10 servings.

Not-to-be-Passed-Over Passover Fudge Brownies

2½ bars (3½ ounces) bittersweet
 chocolate
¼ cup butter
2 eggs

⅛ teaspoon salt
⅔ cup sugar
½ cup cake meal
½ cup walnuts coarsely chopped

1. Melt chocolate and butter over hot water. Cool. Beat eggs and salt until thick and lemon colored.
2. Gradually beat in cooled chocolate mixture.
3. Slowly add cake meal and beat until well blended. Stir in chopped nuts.

4. Spread batter evenly in a well-greased, 8-inch square pan.

5. Bake at 350°F for 35 minutes.

6. Cut into 2-inch squares while still hot.

7. Cool in pan. Devour at great risk to your diet.

Makes 8 servings.

The Seder Apple Strudel Surprise

4 matzahs

1 cup orange juice

½ cup margarine or shortening

2 tablespoons candied orange
    peels

2 cups grated apples

3 eggs, separated

4 tablespoons sugar

2 tablespoons raisins

2 tablespoons chopped almonds
    or walnuts

Cinnamon, nutmeg, and/or
    other seasonings to taste

1. Pour juice into platter. Dip matzahs into juice sufficient to wet; remove immediately.

2. Put 1 matzah into bottom of well-greased 9 × 9 inch baking pan. Make snow of egg whites, beating till stiff.

3. Mix together all other ingredients. Fold in egg whites. Pour ⅓ of batter over matzah in pan. Cover with another matzah. Pour in another ⅓ of batter. Cover with another matzah. Repeat, ending with matzah.

4. Bake 1 hour at 350°F

Makes 9 1-inch square servings.

The "Instead-of-Coffee" Coffee Meringue Cookie

4 large egg whites
¼ tsp salt
1 cup sugar
3 tablespoons instant regular or
    decaf coffee (granules)

1 teaspoon vanilla extract
36 whole coffee beans
    (optional)
Chocolate chips for topping

1. Place oven racks into thirds.
2. Preheat oven to 250°F.
3. Using mixer on high, beat egg whites and salt until foamy.
4. Add sugar one tablespoon at a time, beating until stiff peaks form.
5. Stir in rest of sugar, coffee, and vanilla.
6. Cover 2 baking sheets with parchment paper or waxed paper (using masking tape to attach to baking sheet).
7. Drop tablespoons of batter onto baking sheets.
8. Top with coffee bean or chocolate chip.
9. Sprinkle with cocoa (optional).
10. Bake at 250°F for 2 hours or until dry.
11. Turn oven off, and partially leave oven door open.
12. Leave meringues in oven for another hour.
13. Remove from oven, and carefully remove from paper.
14. Cool completely on oven racks.

Makes 3 dozen cookies.

Scrumptious Strawberry Ice Cream

2 pints strawberries
1 cup sugar

3 egg whites
2 tablespoons lemon juice

1. Wash strawberries; hull and cut into slices.
2. Add sugar and lemon juice; let stand for a while.
3. Beat egg whites until stiff.
4. Fold berries into egg whites, and place in freezer.
5. When partially frozen, take out and beat together. Place back in freezer until firm.

Cookies-to-Go (with the Ice Cream)

½ cup margarine
4 eggs
2 cups cake meal

1 cup chopped walnuts
1 cup sugar

1. Cream margarine and sugar.
2. Beat in eggs, one at a time, until blended.
3. Mix in cake meal and nuts.
4. Form into 1-inch-thick rolls, and wrap in plastic. Refrigerate for 6 hours or overnight.
5. Remove from refrigerator and slice into thin cookies.
6. Bake on lightly greased cookie sheets at 350°F for 12–15 minutes until lightly browned.

The Wise Son's Chosen Chocolate Cake

8 eggs separated
1½ cups sugar
¼ cup orange juice
Rind of 1 orange, grated

2 tablespoons cocoa
¼ cup Passover wine
¾ cup cake meal

1. Grease 2 8-inch square pans and line with waxed paper.
2. Sift the cake meal; beat egg yolks; add sugar and beat until thick and lemony color.
3. Add grated orange rind, cocoa, orange juice, and wine, mixing thoroughly.
4. Gently stir in the sifted cake meal. Beat egg whites until stiff but not dry, and fold into batter.

Pour into prepared pans; bake at 350°F for 40–50 minutes. Turn out on cake rack, and remove waxed paper.

Cut into squares.

Makes a nice size cake for the family.

The Jolly Jelly Nut Cake

5 egg yolks
½ cup sugar
½ cup shortening
1 teaspoon baking powder
1 lemon rind and juice
1¼ cup potato starch

Jelly
5 egg whites
1 cup sugar
½ pound ground nuts
1 teaspoon vanilla

1. Cream sugar and fat.
2. Add egg yolks. Then add baking powder, potato starch and lemon rind.

Put mixture in greased 9 × 12 inch baking pan. Spread jelly on top. Beat egg whites, sugar, nuts, and vanilla; spread on top of jelly; bake at 350°F for 50 minutes or until brown.
Cut into squares.

The Pesach "Spring-Is-Sprung" Compote

¾ cup sugar
1 cinnamon stick
1 vanilla bean, split
1 pound rhubarb, washed, trimmed, tough strings removed with a vegetable peeler, and cut into 1-inch pieces (discard the leaves; they are toxic)

½ cup pitted prunes, halved, if large, quartered
3 blood or navel oranges, or a combination, peeled, white pith and any seeds removed
1 cup (about 5 ounces) fresh raspberries
Fresh mint leaves, for garnish (optional)

1. Place 2 cups of water and the sugar, cinnamon, and vanilla bean in a medium, nonreactive saucepan and bring to a boil.
2. Add the rhubarb and prunes and simmer over low heat, 7–10 minutes. Don't allow it to get too soft—it will "cook" further while macerating.
3. Use a slotted spoon to remove the rhubarb and prunes; then transfer to a large attractive serving bowl.

4. Slice the oranges into thin rounds (if they break apart into little sections after you slice them, that's perfectly fine), and add them, along with the raspberries, to the bowl.

5. Boil the syrup remaining in the saucepan over moderately high heat until reduced by about half.

6. Remove the cinnamon and vanilla bean, and pour the hot syrup over the fruit.

7. Stir well.

8. Let the fruit cool to room temperature; then cover and refrigerate for several hours.

Garnish the compote, if you'd like, with fresh mint leaves.

Makes approximately 10 servings.

My "wish list" for a perfect meal would include_____

_____

_____

_____

_____

_____

_____

_____

_____

_____

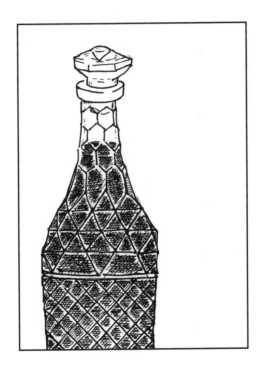

Here's a list of people in our family and their favorite dishes:

Grandma (Mom) _____

Grandpa (Mom) _____

Grandma (Dad) _____

Grandpa (Dad) _____

Uncles: _____

_____

_____

Aunts: _____

_____

_____

Others: _____

_____

_____

Our Family's Culinary Hall of Fame

Let's remember these "Master Chefs" and what they were famous for: _____

_____

_____

_____

_____

These are some recipes that have been handed down for generations in our family:

_____

_____

_____

_____

_____

_____

_____

_____

_____

_____

_____

_____

_____

_____

_____

_____

_____

_____

_____

_____

_____

Some Exotic Passover Trivia

Did You Know That . . . ?

Because of Passover, the Jewish calendar differs from most of the rest of the world. The Christian Western world mainly follows a solar calendar. That makes for a year of 365¼ days—a leap year every four years of an extra day compensating for that annoying little shortfall caused by that quarter. The Moslem Eastern world uses a strictly lunar calendar. That produces a "year" of 354 days, not really in accord with what's happening based on the actual relationship of the earth and the sun. Moslems do nothing to adjust the lunar discrepancy with solar seasons. That's why their holidays as well as the fast days of Ramadan can fall in any season of the year.

Jews are commanded in the Torah to tell time by way of a lunar calendar. Yet the Bible also demands that Passover always be observed as a spring holiday. But what about the shortfall of 11¼ days every year that keeps pushing holidays, with their fixed dates on the calendar, ever backwards? Won't Passover very quickly come out in mid-winter? The solution was to introduce not a leap-year day but an entire month every number of years (seven out of nineteen to be exact, as Talmudic scholars long ago figured out) to "readjust" the lunar calendar with "real" time.

Sure, sometimes Passover will come out "early" on the Western calendar—the earliest possible is March 21. But before long it will be right back where it belongs, at the time when flowers begin to bloom, sometime in mid-April—corresponding to the spring when our people first blossomed like the flowers.

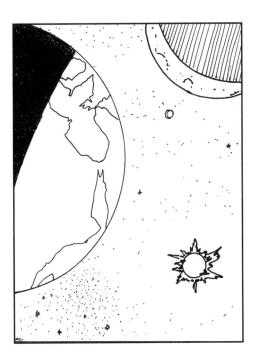

And because Jews have a different calendar, we're also all blessed to have not one but two birthdays—the "English" as well as the Hebrew date we were born—and if you like parties, you're encouraged to celebrate both of them.

After looking up our day of birth on a Hebrew calendar, these are the *two* birthdays for every member of our family: _____

_____

_____

_____

_____

_____

_____

_____

Did You Know That . . . ?

The Number 15 Has Very Special Significance in Judaism

When is Passover on the Jewish calendar? The fifteenth day of the month of Nissan. How many parts are there to the Passover Seder? You won't be surprised if I tell you the answer is 15:

1. Kadesh: The blessing over the wine.
2. Urchatz: Washing the hands.
3. Karpas: Eating a green vegetable.
4. Yachatz: Breaking the middle matzah to be used as the Afikomen.
5. Maggid: Telling the story.
6. Rachtzah: Washing the hands again with a blessing.
7. Motzi: The standard blessing for bread.
8. Matzah: The special blessing for matzah.
9. Maror: Blessing and eating the bitter herbs.
10. Korech: Eating a sandwich of bitter herbs and Charoset.
11. Shulchan Aruch: Eating the festive meal.
12. Tzafun: Finding and eating the hidden Afikomen.
13. Borech: Reciting the blessing after the meal.
14. Hallel: Singing songs of praise.
15. Nirtzah: Praying that everything we have done is acceptable before God.

There is a song that we sing recounting the miracles God performed for us when He redeemed us from Egypt. That song is called *Dayenu* (Enough) for its refrain in which we note that had God done only one of these miracles, "it would have been enough" to earn our eternal gratitude. And sure enough, the song has exactly 15 stanzas.

What accounts for our seeming obsession with this number? Simple. In Hebrew, letters are also numbers. The first letter of the Hebrew alphabet, for example, the *Aleph*, also stands for one. The second letter is two, and so on. That means that

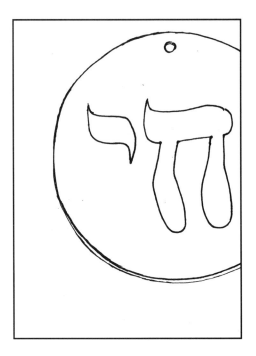

God's name, *Yah* (as in *Hallelu-yah*, praise the Lord) can also be considered a number. Its total of course is none other than 15.

That's why God performed the Passover miracle on the 15th day of the month. It was His way of "signing off" on the miracle, almost like a divine graffiti tag, to guarantee that the Jews realized their deliverance came from God.

And that's also why, on every 15th of a month, Jews remain always a little bit more hopeful. After all, it's the number that represents the mathematical signature of the Almighty!

Jews Believe Just As Some Days Are Lucky, Others Are Unlucky

What is an unlucky day? Try the ninth day of the Hebrew month of Av, known simply as *Tisha B'Av*. Want to know what happened on that day? Don't ask! The list of tragic events is beyond belief.

The first Temple was destroyed by the Babylonians in 586 B.C.E. (before the common era). They surrounded the city, they breached the walls, and they finally succeeded in burning the place regarded by Jews as the holiest spot on earth on the ninth day of Av. Many years later, in 70 C.E. (common era), the Romans fought against Jerusalem's Jewish holdouts and managed, after a lengthy and bitter battle, again to destroy the Temple that had been painstakingly rebuilt. The date when they put the Temple to the torch? The ninth of Av.

In the Middle Ages, Jews were expelled from a number of countries. In 1290, it was England that decreed Jews must leave and picked a date on the secular calendar that Jews were horrified to discover coincided with *Tisha B'Av*. In 1492, the "Golden Age of Spanish Jewry" was brought to a sudden end with the order of Queen Isabella that on a day in the summer selected "at random" by the court, Jews were required to depart en masse. Once again, the date? The ninth of Av. World War I, as Barbara Tuchman's classic work, *The Guns of August*, indicates, started in August—and on *Tisha B'Av*.

How can we explain this peculiar "quirk" of history? The rabbis tell us it's God's way of letting us know *there's no such thing as coincidence—He runs the world!*

**Lucky—and unlucky—days depend on the Hebrew calendar. Here are the Hebrew
dates of some of the most important days of our lives:** _____

_____

_____

_____

_____

_____

_____

_____

Jews from Different Backgrounds and Origins
Celebrate Passover Differently

We may be one people, but in the course of countless centuries, we developed a lot
of different customs. How many kinds of Jews are there? If you go by the stereotype
that for every two Jews there are three synagogues, you might imagine the answer is
in the millions. But that isn't so. Allowing for minor deviations, there are really just
two major groups of Jews: Sephardim and Ashkenazim.

The term Sephardim is derived from the ancient biblical name associated with
Spain. Jews who live in, or whose ancestors came from Spain and Portugal before the
expulsion of the Jews from those countries in 1492 and 1497, respectively, are cul-

turally known as "Sephardim." The term Ashkenazic is derived from "Ashkenaz," which was the medieval Hebrew term for "Germany." Jews who live in, or whose ancestors came from Central or Eastern Europe, are culturally known as "Ashkenazim."

Now here's the really interesting part: *When it comes to Passover, what's kosher for one of these groups isn't kosher for the other.* Ashkenazim accepted a rabbinic stringency many years ago not to eat peas, beans, rice, sesame seeds, and soy products because they were just too close and too indistinguishable from the biblically "forbidden foods" of Passover (leavened bread, cakes, biscuits, crackers, cereal, coffee with cereal derivatives in them, wheat, barley, oats, spelt, rye, and all liquids containing ingredients or flavors made from grain alcohol). Sephardim, in their part of the world, never heard of this decree—just as they never knew of the ban on polygamy that Ashkenazic leaders imposed.

So that's why a Sephardic rabbi might be sitting at his Seder surrounded by all of his wives, serving him his favorite rice and bean dishes—and his Ashkenazi rabbi friend won't even be able to join him for a snack!

There Are Different Kinds of Matzahs—and Not All Matzahs Are Equal

The special "super" version of matzah is known as *shmurah*. That's the Hebrew word for "watched." It means that it was watched from the time it was harvested so that it didn't come into contact with any water that could cause the fermentation process to begin. "Regular" or commercial matzah is "watched" from a much later time, when the wheat is ground into flour.

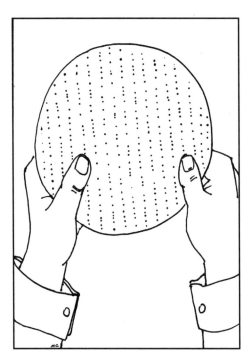

What makes *shmurah* matzah readily recognizable, though, is its shape. Regular matzah, made by machine, is almost invariably in rectangular form. The "super" matzah, baked by hand, is always round. It strives for realism; it wants to look just like the matzah our ancestors took out with them from Egypt. Their bread was round—and the reason why is fascinating. You see, in ancient times, people would make their bread with multiple shapes molded around the edges in ways that symbolized the gods that they worshipped. Since the Hebrews believed that God is eternal, they made their matzah in a rounded shape, which has no beginning or end. Only a symbol of eternity can properly stand for God.

On Passover it's especially important to stress this particular aspect of our belief. There are those who admit there must have been a Creator or the world could not have come into being. But in the aftermath of the Holocaust, a philosophic movement of the twentieth century claimed that "God is dead." The round matzah reminds us that He is alive and well—and always will be.

The Book We Use at the Seder, the Haggadah, Is the Most Frequently Reprinted Book for Jews

That makes sense, on one level, because so many people use it. Passover is the most universally observed holiday by Jews. The Seder is as much for the secular as for the strictly traditional. It has become more than a religious holiday, more even than a national commemoration of peoplehood: it is simply a way of bonding with a commonly shared past, a linking with long-deceased ancestors.

But there is another reason for the Haggadah's popularity. In a religion that had forbidden statues and had little opportunity for artistic expression, the Haggadah allowed for creativity by way of imaginative illustrations accompanying the text.

What should the four different sons—the wise, the wicked, the simple, and the one who does not even know enough to ask—look like? How should the wicked or the wise son be represented? How should we picture angels or Moses or our revered patriarchs and matriarchs? We learn a great deal about Jews in different lands from the way they produced their Haggadahs.

The first printed version of the Haggadah was published in Guadalajara in 1482, just ten years before the expulsion of the Jews from Spain. The first Haggadah printed with illustrations that has come down to us in its entirety was produced in Prague in 1526. This initiated a long line of printed illustrated Haggadot from many different countries, a tradition that continues to this day. Some of the most interesting modern Haggadah editions come from Israel where the importance of the return to Zion predominates as a theme both in the commentary and in the illustrations.

The incredible number of Haggadot printed throughout the years is a prime example of the obsession of the Jews who became known as "The People of the Book" with the printed word.

Books

We have preserved the Book, and the Book has preserved us.
—David Ben-Gurion

If a drop of ink fell at the same time on your book and on your coat, clean first the book and then the garment.   —Talmud

If you drop gold and books, pick up first the books and then the gold.
—Talmud

Books are made for use—not to be hidden away.   —Talmud

Jews are the People of the Book. —Mohammed, the Koran

A good library is a place where the generations meet.   —Niger

A person is known by the books he reads.   —Talmud

To know me is to know the books I have loved. Here are some of the books that have had the greatest impact on my life: _____

_____

_____

_____

_____

_____

_____

_____

In many Jewish homes, additional prayers have been added to the traditional text in order to give expression to some of the modern-day sequels to the Passover story. Passover, after all, proved that God cares about pain and answers our prayers when we cry out to Him in our affliction. What a wonderful opportunity for us, then, to make it more relevant by sharing our hopes for divine intervention in our own times.

One such prayer, recited after the opening paragraph of the Haggadah in which we speak of matzah as the bread of affliction, reads:

Behold this matzah, the symbol of our affliction but also of our liberty. As we look at it, let us remember our brethren everywhere who are in distress. On this festival of our freedom, may our hearts be turned to our brothers and sisters in Arab lands and other places where they are still enslaved, both in spirit as well as in body, and still not able to celebrate this Passover in the traditional, reclining attitude of free men. Rock of Israel, hasten the day when all of our brethren will know true freedom and in consort with the whole house of Israel give thanks to Thee for Thy wondrous deeds and Thy redemption. And may the redeemer come unto Zion.

During the days of Soviet oppression, when Jews suffered severe religious restrictions, world Jewry showed its concern as well as its understanding of collective responsibility by adding a "Matzah of Hope"—a fourth matzah at the Seder table to serve as reminder of those still awaiting fulfillment of Passover's message of freedom and redemption from oppression. On this matzah was recited a commitment to the slaves of our day that "we shall be their voice and our voices shall be joined by all peoples of conscience."

In light of the difficulties faced by many in our days, I would like to add the following prayer at our Passover seder: _____

_____

_____

_____

_____

_____

_____

_____

_____

_____

On Holidays We Have a Biblical Obligation to Be Happy

The Talmud presents us with this ruling: On Passover every head of the household is duty bound to see to it that he, his wife, and his children rejoice, as it is commanded in the Bible: "And you shall rejoice in your feast" (Deuteronomy 16:14).

But how are we supposed to bring this happiness about? The rabbinic answer of old teaches that it depends on the identity of the person seeking happiness. Contemporary students of human behavior may disagree but here is what the ancients, at least, had to say on the matter.

How do men rejoice? With wine and strong drink. It probably wasn't a six-pack, but the fruit of the vine has a long history with happiness.

And what about the women? We'll let others take modern polls, but the Talmud replied: "In Babylonia, with colored garments; in the land of Israel, with ironed linen garments." Fashion and fun, it seems, were partners in old-time feminine joy.

And what of the children? The rabbis advised distributing candies, nuts, and trinkets. Little children probably have changed the least throughout the centuries in their desires.

These are some things we like to do for fun in our family: _____

_____

_____

_____

_____

_____

The Real Reason Why the Jews Were So Hated in Egypt

In all probability it is because the Egyptians couldn't forgive the Jews for doing so much for their country. Joseph, the brilliant young son of Jacob, became Egyptian prime minister as a result of his ability to interpret dreams and to save the Egyptian economy. The Jews were able, smart, and conscientious. And psychologists understand all too well the brilliance of Mark Twain's insight when he said: "I don't know why that man hates me so. I never did anything *for* him."

It's hard to be beholden to those we are forced to acknowledge as benefactors. Perhaps that explains a great deal of the anti-Semitism of the world. Jews are hated because we have just done too much for everybody, so they don't feel comfortable around us.

Chauvinistic and self-serving? Probably. Yet many scholars who have studied the root causes of anti-Semitism believe there is a great deal to it.

There Is One Star Player of the Passover Story Whose Name You'll Never Find in the Entire Book Read at the Seder

Hard to believe but Moses isn't mentioned even once as we retell our tale of the trek from slavery to freedom! How is that possible? Surely, it can't be by coincidence that the man whose name reappears throughout the biblical telling of the story cannot find its way at all into the retelling on the night of Passover. Why this strange anomaly? Commentators explain that it is for the very same reason that God chose to leave no marker on the grave of the greatest Jewish leader, and to this day "no man knows his burial site."

Moses' burial spot remains unknown so that we don't confuse the importance of the messenger with the one who sent him. Moses, great as he was, was but a man. And Jews don't believe that a man is on the same level as God.

Who took us out of Egypt? If we stressed the role of Moses, we'd diminish the real redeemer. Passover is key to the First Commandment in which the Almighty proclaims, "I am the Lord your God who took you out of the land of Egypt and the house of bondage." To make sure we understand this correctly, the rabbis decided to omit Moses' name from the story on the night when God deserves the greatest credit.

There May Be a Fascinating Reason Why Bread Is Forbidden to Be Eaten on Passover

Aside from the fact that it is replaced by matzah, that is.

Yes, the Bible tells us we have to commemorate the story of the Exodus when the Jews didn't have time to let their bread rise and were forced to subsist on matzah. But there is something we ought to remember about the "miracle" of making bread. Yeast is what is used in order to make bread rise. Understanding the power of yeast goes back to ancient Egypt. It wasn't just pyramids that expressed the brilliance of their civilization. The secret of our daily bread goes back to the Egyptian people. Yet, there was a huge dichotomy between their intellect and their moral behavior—as great a gap as demonstrated in modern times by the highly cultured Germans who composed beautiful operas even as they built crematoria.

Perhaps swearing off the product of yeast for one week a year is an actual reminder to the Jewish people that being truly civilized means more than knowing how to "make dough" or to build pyramids.

Passover Has Within It the Wonderful Message That God Is Always Anxious to Offer Us a "Second Chance"

The Jews in the desert had a problem. In order to observe Passover, they knew that one had to be in a state of spiritual purity. But what about those who, for reasons beyond their control, were not fit to observe the Passover holiday? What about those who were far away from home and could not perform the paschal sacrifice? What about all those unexpected circumstances that play havoc with the best of our intentions and make it impossible for us to fulfill something really important to us?

Have no fear. God is compassionate enough to offer us second chances. In the Bible, God decreed: "If any man of you or of your generation shall be unclean by reason of a dead body or be on a journey afar off, he shall keep the Passover of the Lord in the second month on the fourteenth day at dusk" (Numbers 9–11).

The "makeup holiday" has a name. It is called *pesach sheni*—the second Passover. For all those who didn't do it right the first time or who feel that a first failure dooms them forever, it should be heartening and a great comfort to realize that, unlike the common proverb, in life there are indeed second chances.

Some Favorite Parts
of the Haggadah

We Can Learn a Lot from Reciting . . .

This is the bread of affliction which our ancestors ate in the land of Egypt. Whoever is hungry, let him come and eat. Whoever is needy, let him come and celebrate the Passover with us. This year we are here, next year in the land of Israel. This year we are slaves, next year we will be free.

What is the difference between those "who are hungry" and "those who are needy"? There are two different kinds of people that we care about. The first of course is the group that cannot afford food. We have an obligation to make sure that no one suffers the pangs of the stomach. But there is another need that may even be more important. It is not the hunger of the body but the deprivation of the soul.

On Passover we invite both types of people to share with us: the well fed whose lives have no meaning and those who must beg for bread.

Who will derive more from participating in a seder? Strange as it may seem, someone who can afford a luxurious ten-course banquet may find himself fully satisfied for the first time at a meal whose "main dish" is matzah!

We Can Learn a Lot from Reciting . . .

> Why is this night different from any other night? On all other nights, we add leavened bread and matzah; on this night only matzah. On all other nights, we eat every kind of vegetable; on this night only bitter herbs. On all other nights, we do not dip foods even once; on this night, twice. On all other nights, we eat either sitting or reclining; on this night we all recline.

This is the night we encourage our children not simply to read but *to ask*. Judaism is not afraid of questions. Quite the opposite. A religion rooted in mindless obedience is a religion of robots, not of inquiring spirits. "Why" is a word that not only *may* be heard but *must* be heard from the lips of our children.

Isador Isaac Rabi, born into an Orthodox Jewish family, became a Nobel Prize winner in 1944. He attributed his great success to the way in which his mother greeted him every day on his return from school. "Did you," she said, "ask any good questions today?"

Rabi's mother understood what has been part of our tradition for ages. Answers are not as important as questions. Questions open our minds to the true meaning of life and our purpose on earth. To ask is to begin the journey to truth. How exciting it is to hear the youngest child at the Seder begin by asking "Why?"

We were slaves to Pharaoh in Egypt and the Lord our God took us out of there with a strong hand and an outstretched arm. And had the Holy One, blessed be He, not taken our forefathers out of Egypt, then we, our children, and our children's children would still be enslaved to Pharaoh in Egypt.

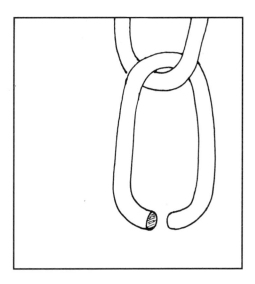

What makes us so sure that had God not redeemed us in the Passover story we would still be slaves? Isn't that a bit far-fetched. Somewhere along the line, wouldn't an Abraham Lincoln have appeared and brought us our freedom?

Yes, of course, we don't literally mean that we would still be building pyramids. What we have in mind is a truth that is far more subtle. Had God not redeemed us then and led us to Sinai, we would to this day be enslaved to the corrupt and immoral way of life that defined great nations like Egypt.

Slavery takes many forms. For those without belief in a Higher Power, it is to be a slave to a mechanistic universe, meaningless and incomprehensible. For those without a divine code of law, it is to be subservient to our animalistic nature and our passions.

God freed us from a way of life that would have defined us to this day were we not privileged to be the beneficiaries of that very first Passover. That's why *we*, not just our ancestors, take such joy in observing this holiday.

> A story of Rabbi Eliezer, Rabbi Yehoshua, Rabbi Elazar son of Azarya, Rabbi Akiva, and Rabbi Tarfon: they were reclining at the Seder in B'nai Brak, and they spent the whole night long telling the story of the going out of Egypt, until their pupils came and said to them, "Our masters, the time has come to recite the morning Shema (Hear O Israel, the Lord is our God, the Lord is One)."

The time for reading the morning Shema is daybreak. It is obvious to all because the room becomes filled with light. Why did the students have to tell their rabbis it was time to fulfill this all-important "mitzvah"? Couldn't they see for themselves?

That is the "hidden" part of the story, the implicit truth that makes this incident

so very meaningful. These rabbis could not know when it was light *because they were in hiding*. These were rabbis forced to gather in a city in which they didn't live—and would normally never have chosen for their Seder, a ritual meant to be observed at home among friends and family. This was a time of Roman persecution, as historians point out. And that is why the Haggadah begins with this tale.

These rabbis had to decide if it was appropriate to celebrate freedom when they themselves were no longer free. It would be a theological problem echoed throughout the ages in every place where the Jews were persecuted. Passover in the Warsaw ghetto? Superficially, that seems absurd. Yet, the rabbis of old and Jews throughout history commemorated the liberation of Passover no matter what their own circumstances. Why? Because Passover is not only a part of our past but also a divine promise of eternal redemption whenever we face the Pharaohs of our history. To celebrate it is to declare that not only did God redeem us long ago, but He will continue to redeem us again.

Rabbi Elazar son of Azarya said: "Behold: I am like a man of seventy."

Rabbi Elazar, we know, was far from seventy at the time. In fact he was all of eighteen years old. Why then did he speak of himself as if he was so much older? The Talmud tells us the full story. The position of Head of the Academy opened up, and the rabbis searched for the most suitable scholar to assume this prestigious position. The very best and brightest was none other than a young man still in his teens. It was Rabbi Elazar, a youth with a beard completely black befitting his age.

What to do? The rabbis hesitated until God intervened with a miracle. Overnight, Rabbi Elazar's beard turned totally white. He now had the bearing and presence of an elderly scholar, and the rabbis could readily appoint him. That's why he said of himself, "I am like a man of seventy."

And why did God bother to make such a miracle? To demonstrate that in choosing our leaders, we ought not to be hung up on their age. Biological years are not as important as personal achievement. There are times when a young man deserves even more respect than those advanced in years.

The Torah speaks of four sons: one who is wise, one who is wicked,
one who is simple, and one who does not even know how to ask.

All children aren't the same. Their differences have to be appreciated—and they can't be treated identically. What's good for one may very well be inappropriate for another. Every good teacher and every smart parent knows this truth: *Train up a child in accord with* his *ways*. Know the child and then respond according to his level of intelligence and maturity.

But why does the Haggadah oppose the wise with the wicked? These aren't really appropriate "opposites". Wise is a description that deals with intelligence. Wicked is a characteristic concerned with ethical behavior. Far more logical, it would seem, ought to be either "wise and foolish" or "righteous and wicked."

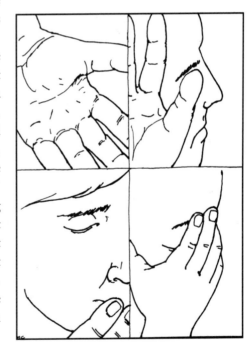

The Haggadah seems to be telling us something, explain the rabbis, about why some children are "wicked." It's not that they're bad. It's just that they aren't wise—they simply haven't been taught. The way to undo wickedness is to shine the light of education and knowledge on their corner of darkness.

Judaism has unlimited faith in the power of learning. A wise son will not be wicked, even as a wicked son only needs to become wise.

> At first our forefathers were idol worshippers, but now the Ever-present One has brought us close to serve Him.

Terach, the father of Abraham, was an idolater, a man who owned a shop that sold "gods" of metal, stone, and wood. But the past didn't dictate the future. Terach's son introduced monotheism to the world, and with Abraham came a new beginning.

Change is possible. The world can be altered by new insights. What was isn't what has to be.

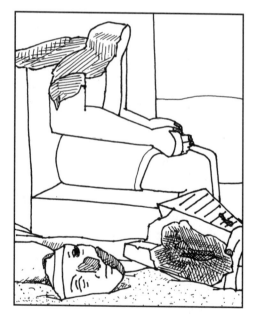

You think that's obvious? It is only because Jews gave this idea to the world. As the Catholic writer Thomas Cahill puts it in *The Gifts of the Jews*, the best-selling study of the Jewish contributions to world civilizations, "Before the Jews it was universally believed that no event is unique, nothing is enacted but once. . . . The Jews were the first people to break out of this cycle. It may be said with some justice that theirs is *the only new idea that human beings had ever*

had! . . . Most of our best words, in fact—new, adventure, surprise, unique, individual, freedom, progress, spirit, faith, hope, justice—are the gifts of the Jews." After all that, don't you feel like celebrating?

> And this is what stood for our fathers and for us—because not just one rose up against us to destroy us. Rather, in every generation they rise up against us to destroy us, but the Holy One, Blessed is He, saves us from their hand.

Are Jews paranoiacs? Do we suffer from a delusion that "the whole world is out to get us"? Perhaps it seems that the Jewish obsession with anti-Semitism must be far out of proportion to reality. Yet, as Henry Kissinger once sharply pointed out, even paranoiacs can have real enemies. And history seems to validate the observation at the Seder that "in every generation they rise up to destroy us."

How can we explain the obsession of the world with Jews who represent less than one quarter of one percent of the earth's population? Why are Jews hated even in lands where no Jews live? Why were Jews the target of the world's first genocide?

The best place to search for an answer is in the writings of the man who made "The Final Solution" his life's mission. Adolf Hitler managed to murder six million and planned for the extermination of every single Jew. What motivated him? Here is how he put it in *Mein Kampf*: "The Jews must be destroyed because they have inflicted on the world the idea of conscience. This is a Jewish invention. The war for domination of the world is waged only between these two camps alone—the Germans and the Jews."

That is why "The Holy One, Blessed be He, saves us from their hand." The mission of the Jew is to serve, as Isaiah said, as "a light unto the nations." As long as we fulfill our divine task, God has a strong personal interest in ensuring our survival.

And these are the ten plagues that the Holy One brought against the Egyptians in Egypt: blood, frogs, lice, wild beasts, pestilence, boils, hail, locusts, darkness, slaying of the firstborn.

What are the total number of plagues? Ten. And the total number of commandments? Also ten.

What links these two? What message was God trying to convey by the numeric correspondence of laws and of plagues? The *Midrash* explains it this way: Mankind is always given a choice. Obey God and the moral code of Sinai or suffer the consequences.

There is humor in the approach of some liberal thinkers that at Sinai God gave the Jews the "Ten Suggestions." But of course that isn't what happened. God didn't offer us options; He presented us with commandments. To obey the laws against theft, murder, adultery, as well as the other seven is to commit to a lifestyle that acknowledges divine demands on our behavior. Disregard the laws of these ten, the rabbis remind us, and know that another set of ten will surely follow.

Oh, and one more thing, adds the *Midrash*: This idea of the ten is so important that God wants it to stare us in the face every time we take a look at our hands, the hands that we use in carrying out our actions. "Why did God create us with ten fingers?" the rabbis ask, not as a biological but as a theological question. So that our fingers remind us always to choose between blessing and punishment, they answer.

> If He had taken us out of Egypt and not executed judgments upon them, it would have been sufficient for us.

We celebrate Passover not because of the death of our enemies but because of our redemption. Yes, God did drown the Egyptians and that was perfectly justified. Divine punishment, the Talmud teaches, follows the principle of "measure for measure." As people do, so is done to them. The Egyptians had been particularly cruel to the Jews and cast their children into the river. That's why they met their deaths in exactly the same manner. But that was God's decision. It is He who took the lives of these wicked people. Jews were aware of what happened to those who caused them so much grief, but that wasn't going to make them smile. When human beings die it is sad, no matter how much they deserved their fate.

Not once after all the wars Israel won did Jews schedule a victory parade with music and dancing. They always explained that victories that included victims didn't warrant celebrations. As the famous story has it, many years ago a palace official insulted Hasdai Ibn Shaprut, a Jewish advisor to the king of Spain. The king told Hasdai he should have the offender's tongue removed. Instead of carrying out this cruel punishment, Hasdai befriended his enemy. When asked why he didn't do what the king ordered, he replied: "But I did. I removed his tongue that spoke ill of me and replaced it with a tongue of kindness." Far better to turn enemy into friend than to harm him!

> In every generation, each individual is obligated to see himself as if he actually went out of Egypt, as it is written: "And you shall tell your son on that day, 'Because of this did God do wonders for me when I went out of Egypt.'" The Holy One Blessed is He redeemed not only our forefathers. He redeemed us with them as well.

Minor surgery, Mel Brooks once famously said, is an operation on somebody else; major surgery is any procedure, no matter how small, that is done on me.

Passover tells a story that happened long ago. If it's repeated as an event that affected others, at the most it can only be interesting. If it's a story that happened to me, it's life altering. Just imagine if I hadn't survived, I can tell listeners: my children and grandchildren wouldn't be here.

That is in fact true about the exodus from Egypt. Had God not taken our ancestors out, brought them to Mount Sinai to accept the Torah and then continued them on to Israel to create our collective national consciousness, neither my family nor I would be here today. Perhaps we would be alive. But we would assuredly not be who we are. We might live but never realize the true purpose of life. That gives us the ability not just to retell but to relive the story. We feel it as strongly as if it happened to us. Because in a certain sense, it did.

Praise the Lord, all nations! Laud Him, all peoples! For great is the kindness that He has shown us and His truth endures forever. Praise God!

"In the beginning God created the heavens and the earth." God, if He is to have meaning as the Creator, is universal. Jews may for the time being be the only ones who accept Him and His Torah. The vision for the end of days, however, is of a time when all nations praise the Almighty and abide by His will.

That dream has a name. It is called the days of the Messiah. Judaism would be incomplete if it didn't lay out the hope and the possibility for a world free from the ravages of war, a time when people would turn their spears into pruning hooks and their swords into plowshares.

Why, ask the rabbis, did history decree that Jews be scattered round the world? It is no accident, they suggest. It is part of God's divine plan to have His people, by their presence, spread the knowledge of God to the four corners of the earth.

As we come to the closing portion of the Haggadah and the end of the Seder, we need to remind ourselves that God isn't fully served if only a small portion of His children acknowledge Him. Jews must set the example and serve as mankind's teachers. Then the day will come when *all* nations will join in praising the Lord.

Next Year in Jerusalem.

What is it about Jerusalem that captures the imagination of the Jews? Why is Jerusalem so important that wherever a Jew prays around the world he must face in its direction? Why does every Jew conclude not only the Seder but the Day of Atonement, Yom Kippur, with the response *Next Year in Jerusalem*?

Jerusalem is the city of David. It is a place of great beauty: "Ten measures of beauty came down to earth; nine were taken by Jerusalem, and one by the rest of the world," note the rabbis. It is also a city of great spirituality. It is where Jews came to worship in the first as well as the second Temple, revered as the holiest site on earth. The Temples were destroyed but what they represent still gives life to the Jews to this day. Without the inspiration of that long gone place, Judaism would be an orphan, devoid of its spiritual source.

In the words of the Talmud, "As the heart in the midst of the body, so is Jerusalem situated in the midst of the inhabited earth." Don't be surprised, then, if you live to witness the fulfillment of the biblical prophecy that "Jerusalem is destined to become the metropolis of the world." And that may very well be because, as Israel Zangwill explained it, "Jerusalem, like Heaven, is more a state of mind than a place."

> Who knows one? I know one. One is our God who is in heaven and earth. Who knows two? I know two. Two are the tablets of the covenant.

One God gave us two tablets. But why? Couldn't God have written all ten commandments on one tablet? What was the point of dividing them into two groups, five on each tablet as if they were separate laws?

The answer, the Talmud explains, is because God wanted to make a profoundly new and all-important statement about the true meaning of religion. There are those who limit divine concern to matters that refer only to our relationship with God. But that is not an accurate summary of religious responsibility. God demands not only allegiance to Him but also ethical behavior toward our fellow human beings. What we do in response to our neighbors is just as *religious* a statement as how we worship God.

Look at the ten commandments carefully, and you will see that the first five all revolve around laws between man and God. All of them, in fact, contain God's name. The second tablet, however, does not mention God even once. It is an elaboration of

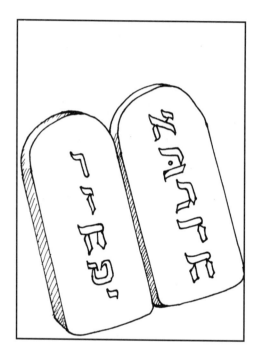

the biblical ideal to "Love your neighbor as yourself." *Both* tablets are the essence of Jewish belief. One without the other is schizophrenic religion. And at the Seder I emphasize that I know the meaning not only of one—my God—but also two, the God who insists that because I worship Him I also respect those created in His image.

One kid, one kid, that my father bought for two zuzim, one kid, one kid. Then came a cat and ate the kid my father bought. . . . Then came a dog and bit the cat. . . . Then came a stick and hit the dog. . . . Then came a fire and burned the stick. . . . Then came water and put out the fire. . . . Then came a bull and drank the water. . . . Then came the slaughterer and slaughtered the bull. . . . Then came the Angel of Death and slew the slaughterer. . . . Then came the Holy One, Blessed is He, and slaughtered the Angel of Death.

The Seder closes with what seems to be a little nursery rhyme that speaks, of all things, about a "kid," a small goat purchased by a father for "two zuzim", two coins of ancient currency. Of course the closing prayer is a parable. The "kid"? The Jewish people. The father? Our Father in heaven. How did He acquire us? With the "two zuzim," symbolic of the two tablets on which were inscribed the ten commandments. And who are the cat, the dog, the stick, the fire, as well as all the other symbols that follow? The various empires that each played a role on the scene of world history, gaining control for a while only to be conquered by another mighty nation that took its place.

Is this then the way it will go on forever? Are we destined to witness the rise and fall of endless rulers with no final resolution? Passover promises us a better end. God will come and slay the Angel of Death as well as all those who stood in the way of the establishment of His Kingdom. On Passover we also declare our belief that that day is near!

Passover Round the World

Jews Celebrate Passover Even in . . .

Jews in the Diaspora

The Jews of the Passover story were Jews in exile. Egypt was not the home promised by God to the descendants of Abraham. The Hebrews had come to a foreign land because of a famine. Viewed as strangers, they soon found themselves enslaved.

Passover commemorates their redemption. Those who left Egypt and their children founded a nation in the land of Canaan, today known as Israel. Yet history did not allow God's chosen people to rest comfortably in the land once they inherited it. Numerous times the Jews had to cope with expulsion, exile, and wandering over the face of the earth. Jews settled in countries that at first welcomed them, only most often to be subsequently banished after years of persecution.

The memory of Egypt remained alive throughout all of these years of exile. Jews celebrated Passover in commemoration of God's concern, compassion, and intervention in the ancient time of their misery. All the while, they wondered why a God who redeemed them once long ago, allowed them again to endure so much suffering.

Forced to live in the Diaspora, scattered across the globe far from their ancestral home, Jews had to contend with the ultimate theological problem: Why didn't God send another Moses and redeem them once more from all the places of their dispersion?

Jewish scholars came up with but two possible answers: The first was that God's silence could only be attributed to Jewish sin. The relationship between God and the Jews is covenantal and conditional. God wouldn't take care of His children if they disobeyed the divine rules as set down at Mount Sinai. To bring about another Passover, Jews themselves would have to prove themselves worthy by renewing their commitment to Torah and to Jewish life. Passover in this perspective represents the ultimate challenge: changing not God's dealings with us but our behavior toward Him.

Jewish tradition, however, offers another possibility to explain why history has imposed so many centuries of wandering on the people who are supposedly God's favorites. Jews were given a mission. The prophets called it being in the service of God "as a light unto the nations." It is not only we who need God, but, strikingly enough, it is also God who needs us. God requires a paradigm of spirituality, a universal illustration of what is possible when human beings take upon themselves a commitment to make their lives a mirror of the image of God. *The role of the Jew is to be a divine representative of the holy.*

For that reason, and not because of their sinfulness, it became the divine plan to scatter the Jews over the entire world. The Midrash puts it this way: A farmer takes his finest seeds and does not restrict them to one small portion of his acreage. He wants the best to take root everywhere. He casts them to the wind in the hope that their magnificence will take root wherever they find a resting place.

No one can be sure which of the two explanations is the correct one for Diaspora Jewry. All we know is that to this day we still find ourselves in many different lands. And like the Jews of Egypt of old, we remember the blessings of the past and pray that they serve as a harbinger for the future.

Jews celebrate Passover in some of the most exotic and unexpected places on earth. Customs differ. Foods vary. Texts tell the story in different ways. But Jews everywhere share the bonds with a link to common ancestors and a firm belief in a divine Ruler committed to justice, mercy, and the fulfillment of his messianic promise.

Jews Celebrate Passover Even in . . .

Yemen, Among the Locust Eaters

In the biblical book of Leviticus, the Bible mentions four species of locusts that are kosher to eat. In most of the world, Jews forgot how to identify these types. It just never seemed important enough to want to remember. But in Yemen, South Arabia, the religious authorities among Jews made sure to pass this information along from generation to generation. That's because locusts are a staple of that part of the world's diet, widely prized and heavily consumed.

Yemen is believed to be the birthplace of the Arab people. Yemen was the home of the legendary Queen of Sheba who paid a famous visit to King Solomon when she heard he was "the wisest of all men." Jews came to Yemen before the destruction of the first Temple prior to the sixth century before the common era. In fact, Yemen is one of the few countries that was governed by Jewish monarchs. King Abu Karib Asad converted to Judaism in the fourth century, as did Dhu Newas who ruled a century later.

Most of the Jews who lived in Yemen have emigrated to Israel in modern times. But the ruler of Yemen, Saif al-Islam Ahmad allowed the Jews of Yemen to leave only on one condition: That they first teach their crafts to the Muslims.

Today there are perhaps five hundred Jews left in Yemen. Over two hundred thousand presently reside in their ancient homeland of Israel. For them Passover is far more than a holiday of the past. It commemorates the most important moments of their contemporary redemption as well.

Yemenite Jews have a special custom at the first Seder. They sprinkle their clothing with incense. For centuries they believed this was a fitting sign they would soon be coming to the Holy Land that they wanted to enter smelling their very best. It is a custom that gives real meaning to the phase, "the sweet smell of success."

The Caucasian Mountains, with Spears and Daggers

A proverbial blessing among Jews for a long life has always been phrased: "May you live until one hundred and twenty." That's because Moses, the greatest Jew, lived to that ripe old age, and we don't feel it's right to wish anyone a longer life than the rabbi considered the greatest Jew who ever lived.

But there is one place on earth where people do live even longer, at least one of them to a recorded one hundred thirty-five years of age. We don't really know if it's the yogurt, the clean air of the mountains, or the fact that there are no "couch potatoes" among these rugged people, but Daghestan, "land of mountains" in Turkish, made its Jewish residents not only super healthy but also Superman strong.

Daghestani Jews trace their presence there back to at least the year 80 B.C.E. In their society, in order to survive, they glorified not the scholar but rather the warrior. Pride came not from carrying around a book but rather a pistol or sword that they brought with them even when they went to synagogue to pray.

At the Seder on the night of Passover, families sit around dressed in what they call their "liberty clothes," adorned by a short spear at their sides. They arrange themselves in formations just like soldiers resting after a major battle. And on the night of Passover they explain that they are strong and mighty, not simply because of their weapons. They affirm that their greatest strength is their faith in God who redeemed the Jews from Egypt long ago. To close their Seder, they recite in unison: "May it be the will of God that the Messiah, of the Son of David, come and bring redemption to all the people in exile, as the Lord our God has redeemed our ancestors in time of old."

Morocco, Where They Have Lived—in the Western Part of North Africa—Since Ancient Times

Ruled by many different peoples, primarily the Arabs and the French, Moroccan Jewry has maintained the customs of its ancestors with scrupulous care and precision.

Moroccan Jews are world famous for their craftsmanship, especially in jewelry making. They are especially noted for their creativity and elegant workmanship in creating gold and silver jewelry as Jewish holy objects.

Their celebration of Passover is especially renowned with the magnificence of their outfits. In the Bible, the Jews were commanded to prepare their dress for a long journey. Moroccan Jews have always stressed their readiness to welcome the Messiah when He comes and to immediately begin their crossing to Israel.

After the close of the Passover holiday, Moroccan Jews have their own special rite that they call the *Mimouna* festivities. Mimouna is a celebration of liberty, of community values, of friendship and of togetherness, and most important of all, it is a remarkable opportunity to demonstrate Moroccan hospitality. Jews open their doors and set a festive table for neighbors, friends, and family. Distinctive foods and dress dominate. In contrast to the Seder night when everyone rushes home from synagogue to begin the family service, Mimouna allows the entire community the time to share food and drink as well as the special blessings for *tababah*—success. Because Passover is a spring holiday, Moroccan Jews always added that Mimouna is a wonderful time for courting and looking for a future bride or groom. Singles would mingle under the watchful eyes of their parents.

As a closing tribute to the holiday, the morning after Mimouna, families in coastal villages would get up and head for the seashore, splash their faces with water, and step barefoot into the ocean to replay the miraculous crossing of the Red Sea. Those living inland have the custom of going to the local lakes, springs, or swimming holes and symbolically reenacting the Passover miracle.

Although scholars are not sure of the origin of the word *mimouna*, many believe it comes from the name Maimon, father of Maimonides. Maimon lived in the City of Fez where the Mimouna originated and where he died—on the day after Passover.

Afghanistan, Where the Famous "*Tallit*-Men" Made Their Home

According to Islamic legend, the prophet Ezekiel settled in the Afghani City of Balk, which according to their tradition is the oldest city in the world. The present-day City of Hazara is probably the place mentioned by Ezra the Scribe as the refuge for some of the lost ten tribes.

A modern-day scholar born in Kabul who has done extensive research on the history of Afghani Jews has noted that many customs in Afghanistan today can be traced back to Judaic roots. Many Afghanis wear a scarf-like cloth striped like a *tallit*. In addition, they often shave their heads, but leave the side *payot*. Some light candles and drink grape juice on Friday night, without knowing any reason for it. Others have a tradition of having elders teach them on Saturday, in contrast to Friday that is the Muslim day of rest.

A contemporary Jerusalem rabbi, Eliyahu Avichayil, searching out lost Jewish communities around the world, found that Pathin women wear amulets with the words *Shema Yisrael* (Hear, O Israel) and light candles on Friday before sundown.

Afghani Jews had a Seder custom specific to them. The leader of the Seder lifted the bone from the Seder plate and stressed its meaning as a symbol of "God's outstretched arm." Afghani Jews made it the highlight of their observance and would always stress that God's outstretched arm would be extended once more to deliver them from a land in which they no longer felt welcome.

Before the Soviet invasion in 1979, there were only thirty Jews remaining who had not emigrated to Israel. Recently, newspapers reported the remarkable story of the last two Jews left. According to the Associated Press, Zebulon Simeontov, forty-two, and Ishaq Levin, in his seventies, "lived at separate ends of the same decaying synagogue in the Afghan capital and are feuding, each claiming to be the rightful owner of the synagogue and its paraphernalia. 'I begged him not to be my enemy,' Mr. Levin says referring to his co-religionist. 'If I die tomorrow, who will bury me in the traditions of my religion?'" How sad an ending to a story of contemporary redemption.

The Surviving Jewish Communities of Poland

A long time ago Poland was in the vanguard of those countries that understood a Jewish presence would be a wonderful blessing for their land. When in the fifteenth and sixteenth centuries Jews were expelled from many European countries, Poland welcomed the talented outcasts and offered them unheard of rights.

Today Polish Jewry is far more remembered for Auschwitz and its hostility to the Jews during the Holocaust. Jews did observe Passover even when they found themselves encircled and doomed in the Warsaw Ghetto. It was the Jews during those horrific days who created a new prayer that best captured the Passovers of modern-day slavery.

The following was recited in a concentration camp, written by a rabbi who knew that if the Jewish prisoners would abstain from leavened products on their Passover, they would truly die of starvation. The prayer was:

"Our Father in heaven, it is known to you that it is our wish to do your will and to celebrate Passover by eating matzah and not eating *chametz*. But our hearts are pained because of our enslavement that prevents us from fulfilling your will. We are in danger of our lives. Behold, we are ready to fulfill your commandment, 'And you shall live by my laws and not die by them.' We pray to you that you may keep us alive and redeem us soon so that we may observe your laws with a perfect heart, amen."

Ethiopia, Where They Take Literally the Words of Solomon That Black Is Beautiful

Ethiopian Jews, known as *falashas*, according to a legend recorded by the historian Josephus in the second century, may even be direct descendants of Moses from the time he served as a general in the Egyptian army fighting a war against Ethiopia. It was then that, according to one story, Moses took an Ethiopian princess as a bride and became for a time an Ethiopian ruler.

Before the advent of Christianity, at least half the inhabitants of Ethiopia worshipped the "God of Moses." Ethiopian Christians to this day reflect the tremendous influence of Judaism on their culture. An Ethiopian church requires male circumcision on the eighth day after birth; forbids the eating of pork; requires that Saturday be observed as a day of rest in addition to Sunday; reckons the calendar from Adam and Eve, not from the birth of Jesus; and builds its churches on the plan of King Solomon's temple.

Until Ethiopian Jewry emigrated to Israel in a stunning operation code-named Operation Moses in 1984, Ethiopian Jews observed Passover almost in the very way it had been celebrated in the time of the Bible. On the eve of Passover, with the setting of the sun, the entire community assembled in the court of the synagogue and offered a paschal lamb on the altar. After the sacrifice was slaughtered and roasted, the meat was eaten with unleavened bread according to the details laid out in the book of Exodus.

Throughout their stay in Ethiopia, Jews realized why they were called *falashas*. *Falasha*, in the tongue of the G'ez, means stranger. No matter that the Jews had lived among their countrymen for thousands of years. As Jews they were still strangers. That is why Passover remained so meaningful to them. Ethiopian Jews are no longer *falashas*; the Passover of modern times has turned strangers into Israeli citizens.

It's important to know our roots. These are the countries from which our ancestors came: _____

_____

_____

_____

_____

_____

_____

_____

These are some Passover customs that are special to our family: _____

_____

_____

_____

_____

_____

_____

_____

_____

_____

Afterword: A Family Legacy

Throughout the ages, many Jews carried on a remarkable tradition. Parents would write what they called a "Last Will" to their children. This will was unlike any other. It did not specify what children were to inherit. Its concern was not financial; it did not deal with the distribution of wealth after death. Jewish history records countless instances of ethical wills, reflecting a desire on the part of older generations to share hard-earned lessons, to pass on their spiritual acquisitions, not their material goods.

This, they wanted to tell their children, is who I was and this is what I learned in my years on earth. This is the greatest legacy I can leave. This is how I want to be remembered.

These wills are among the most moving of family documents. For many, their value was in fact far more than any treasures of gold and silver. Perhaps in the most meaningful sense of all, they accomplished the near impossible: they allowed their authors a measure of immortality.

Today our harried life styles do not encourage writing letters or leave time for lengthy, intimate conversations. Do our children really know who we are? And will our future generations have any sense of our lives, our hopes, our dreams—and our uniqueness?

It is hoped this book will serve to accomplish some of these goals. It is a book whose authorship is shared between us. On many pages, I wanted only to be the catalyst for your thoughts. What you wrote down there is a self-portrait that no one else could have drawn. It turns this book into a reflection of *you*—and makes it the most personal book ever written.

I urge you to think carefully about what you transmit on these pages. It represents your legacy. Give the book to those you love the most. And trust me: someday this book will be treasured among the most valuable items in their possession.

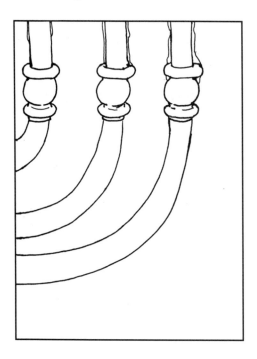

The most important ideas I want to leave to my descendants as my legacy are:

_____

_____

_____

_____

_____

_____

_____

A family tree can wither if no one knows its roots.   —Jewish proverb

This is a family tree of our ancestors: _____

_____

_____

_____

_____

_____

_____

_____

_____

Our Family Memory Page

Remembering Our Dearest
Friends and Family

Friendship marks a life even more deeply than love. Love risks
degenerating into obsession, friendship is never anything but sharing.
—Elie Wiesel

These are the people who shared Passover with us: _____

_____

_____

_____

_____

_____

_____

_____

_____

_____

_____

_____

Appendix: Passover Resources

For lists of Passover approved products:

The Union of Orthodox Jewish Congregations makes available for every year a complete and revised list of Passover-approved products. Contact them at www.ou.org, call 212-563-4000, or write 11 Broadway, New York, NY 10004.

For beginners who want to know more about holiday basics, see:

Judaism 101 at www.jewfaq.org or www.chabad.org.

For a list of the twenty best Passover sites on the web, see Judaism.about.com.

For audio presentations about Passover, see www.613.org

For interesting essays and commentaries on Passover, see www.torah.org

To send free Passover cards by e-mail, see cards.123greetings.com

For a Passover Kid's Fun Book, with games, puzzles, fill-ins, mazes, word games, cartoons and pages to color, see www.santacruzhag.com

For a great link to 118 other websites about Passover, try www.maven.co.il

Acknowledgments

Rabbi Blech would like to thank his agents Rita Battat Silverman and Laura Kossoff at Dream Weavers Management, and Bob Shuman, Amanda Rouse, and Bonnie Fredman at Citadel Press.

About the Author

Rabbi Benjamin Blech is an internationally recognized educator, religious leader, author and lecturer. He is the author of ten highly acclaimed books, a number of which are used as basic texts in colleges and Jewish Day Schools around the country. A recipient of the American Educator of the Year Award, he is an Associate Professor of Talmud at Yeshiva University as well as the Rabbi Emeritus of the Young Israel of Oceanside congregation. In a national poll, he was recently ranked #16 among the 50 most influential Jews in America.